Everyday Wisdom

365 ways to a better you

Everyday Wisdom

365 ways to a better you

Susannah Marriott

Illustrated by Michelle Tilly

An Hachette UK Company
First published in Great Britain in 2011 by Spruce
a division of Octopus Publishing Group Ltd
Endeavour House, 189 Shaftesbury Avenue
London, WC2H 8JY
www.octopusbooks.co.uk
www.octopusbooksusa.com

Distributed in the US by
Hachette Book Group USA
237 Park Avenue
New York, NY 10017 USA

Distributed in Canada by
Canadian Manda Group
165 Dufferin Street
Toronto, Ontario, Canada, M6K 3H6

Produced by **Bookworx**
Editorial Jo Godfrey Wood
Design Peggy Sadler

ISBN 13 978-1-84601-333-1
ISBN 10 1-84601-333-X

A CIP catalogue record for this book is available from the British Library.

Printed and bound in China.

10 9 8 7 6 5 4 3 2

Author's acknowledgments
Thanks to Georgina Brown for the scent meditation; Elfréa Lockley for thoughts on writing; and the Muses, Amanda Brown for the resources meditation and her constant inspiration, Farzana Patel for the apple tree tale, and Richard Bell for sketchbook inspiration – www.wildyorkshire.co.uk/naturediary

Contents

Introduction 6
How to use this book 8

Days 1 to 31 10
Checklist 1 40
Days 32 to 61 42
Checklist 2 70
Days 62 to 92 72
Checklist 3 102
Days 93 to 122 104
Checklist 4 132
Days 123 to 152 134
Checklist 5 162
Days 153 to 182 164
Checklist 6 192
Days 183 to 212 194
Checklist 7 222
Days 213 to 242 224
Checklist 8 252
Days 243 to 273 254
Checklist 9 284
Days 274 to 303 286
Checklist 10 314
Days 304 to 334 316
Checklist 11 346
Days 335 to 365 348
Checklist 12 378

Conclusion 380

Introduction

What is wisdom? This little book urges you to explore the numerous paths leading toward greater understanding. Month by month, in manageable steps, you will explore the wisdom of the body and the self, finding out what mindful movement and instinct can teach you about yourself and your approach to life, and how exercise optimizes brain function. You will also experience the many ways in which tuning in to the wisdom of the mind and the heart reveals essential truths and the self-knowledge, reflection or meditation that comes from many ancient traditions.

Along the way, learn from other forms of wisdom: religious insight, the innate knowledge of nature and more conventional learning, too, such as techniques to sharpen concentration and attention span and make you more money-wise, street-savvy and productive at work.

Try to do each day's task as it arrives and the effects will build up incrementally. Some tasks are very practical: yoga poses, breathing exercises or cooking tips. Other tasks ask you to enquire into your emotional life, relationships and motivation and to start thinking about how you can change them for the better. If you struggle with a task,

don't worry, try again tomorrow or decide to skip this entry. You might like to jot down your feelings at the back of each section.

Scattered among the practical exercises are profound thoughts to contemplate, gathered from great thinkers whose teachings and actions have changed the way we see the world, from Ancient Greek philosophers to Mahatma Gandhi. Religious thinkers, including early Christian mystics and Sufi poets, are reflected here, as are poets such as William Wordsworth and William Blake. And, at the end of each month, 'teaching tales' introduce the legendary quests many mythical figures have undertaken in order to become wise.

I hope you emerge from this journey with a heightened awareness of what makes you tick, more considered reactions and judgments and a new-found appreciation of your place in our wonderful world and the boundless opportunities waiting out there for you.

How to use this book

If you've bought this book as part of your plan for the New Year, that's fine, but if you've picked this book up at some time during the middle of the year, don't worry. It will still work for you. You don't have to start it on New Year's Day; you can start any time you feel like it during the year. Just turn to Day 1 and work your way through the days in order. You will find that the months have either 30 or 31 days to reflect the real year, so you might want to match the month you're in with one that has the correct number of days on offer (the first month has 31 days).

At the end of every month you'll find a page for assessing how you're getting on. This serves as an opportunity to think about what you've read and whether any of the ideas are working for you. There's also a space here to write down your thoughts and think about how you're getting on. Run out of writing space? Turn to the final pages of the book and you'll find more pages to continue any important personal notes.

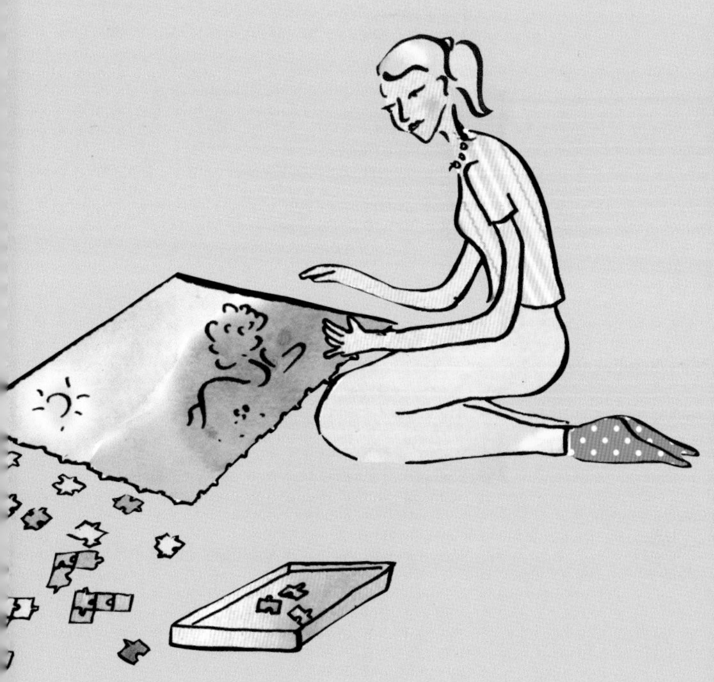

1 Light-bulb moments

Wise thought

YOUR NOTEBOOK
You are more likely to jot down thoughts if you love the design of your notebook and relish the feel of your pen on the paper, so invest in good-quality products.

By definition, epiphanies, sudden life-changing revelations or illuminating thoughts, strike at the most inopportune or mundane moments. It's worth taking notice of them because through them you can acquire wisdom.

Make sure you preserve your epiphanies for later reflection by carrying a notebook and pen at all times. To witness characters experiencing such special moments of insight, read James Joyce's collection of short stories, *Dubliners*.

Stop the world

2

It's easy to live like a mouse on a wheel: you go to work, you eat, you sleep, you go to work again, and so on, and then it's the weekend. Make regular time to step off that wheel and reflect on your life.

Today, spend a few minutes daydreaming on your commute to work. Don't interrogate yourself during this downtime; simply let thoughts emerge and listen to what your innate wisdom is telling you.

Instant wisdom

ESTEEM BOOST
Wisdom equates with good self-esteem; to boost yours instantly, get your hair cut or try out a new tint shade.

3 Open your eyes

There is wisdom all around us, but usually we're far too distracted by work or our hectic home lives to take much notice. To wake up your innate powers of perception, close your eyes and take a few slow breaths in and out.

Open your eyes and find an object in the foreground. Observe its texture, the way the light hits it, the materials it is made from. Blink, then look into the middle distance. Choose an object in the middle distance and repeat the observation. Finally, repeat with a distant object.

List the things you love

4

Remind yourself of your passions to ignite your inner vision, which in turn will enhance your inner wisdom. What gives you that pit-of-the-stomach energy, enthusiasm and clear-sightedness? Dancing? Gardening? Watching your favorite football team? The songs of The Clash?

Write a list of the things you love doing and pin it somewhere where you will often see it. This will remind you to schedule these activities into your life more frequently.

5 Stand tall

Instant wisdom

STRUCTURE IS GOOD FOR WISDOM

Choose structured garments that inspire you to stand tall instead of shapeless clothes that encourage you to slump.

Presenting yourself to the world with confidence convinces others that you have experience and faith in your own judgment and wisdom; whether this is actually true or not.

Whenever you remember today, lift your breastbone, lengthen the back of your neck and look into the middle distance as you walk. This adds to your stature and gives authority to your gait.

Sensory recall

6

To cultivate your memory and perception skills, so that you can add to your wisdom, try this version of an age-old party game. Gather together an assortment of unconnected everyday objects. Look for items with different textures, colors and associations, such as a scented candle, a feather or leaf, a mirror, a sprig of lavender or a photograph.

Place the items on a tray and pick them up one by one, looking at them from all angles, running your fingers over their different textures and smelling their scents.

Now put the tray away and try to write a list of the objects. When you struggle to remember, close your eyes and try to recall the visual details, scents and textures.

Thinking is more interesting than knowing, but less interesting than looking.

Goethe

7

Plant mint for wisdom

Mint is a brain stimulant that thrives for even the least green-fingered gardener. To ensure you have a ready supply on hand when you need it, plant mint in large pots or in a herb patch near your door (it's best to plant it in pots otherwise it will take over your garden).

There are various varieties to choose from: spearmint, peppermint, pineapple, ginger and lemon mint. Why not run your hands over the leaves as you leave home to give you instant mental stimulation?

Be here more often

8

People who meditate have always been considered wise and going inside yourself gives you a chance to be truly still in your busy life. Research shows that meditation improves attention span, focused awareness and memory.

During meditation you maintain awareness of the present moment, which frees the mind, momentarily, from the emotional roller-coaster provided by thoughts of the past and future. This respite ushers in a sense of expansiveness and heightened self-knowledge. At some point today, while you are pouring coffee, dressing a child or brushing your teeth, focus totally on 'now' and let 'then' be.

From meditation springs wisdom.
The Buddha

9 Think a wise thought

Take a long walk today (aim for 20–30 minutes), keeping up a pace that leaves you slightly breathless, but able to carry on a conversation or sing a song to yourself. At the halfway point notice how thoughts are becoming more reflective and home in on a single wise thought:

I only went out for a walk and finally concluded to stay out till sundown, for going out, I found, was really going in.

John Muir

Take a walk

10

Moving the body seems to stimulate brain cells to grow and connect with each other and aerobic exercise really does make you wiser and brainier.

Brisk walking is one of the safest ways to start if you are new to working out. Easy ways to add brain-stimulating steps to your day today include getting off the bus one stop early or walking up the escalator or stairs instead of taking the elevator.

Instant wisdom

STRESS-FREE WALK
When you drive to the supermarket, turn into a parking space as far from the store as possible. It's less stressful and you get a good walk there and back.

11 Wake up your brain

Try this cross-patterning exercise to help the both left and right side of your brain to talk to each other. You will create instant brain-enlivening activity and long-term wisdom.

Cross your arms and catch your earlobes between the thumbs and index fingers of your opposite hands. Give a brief squeeze, then change the cross of your arms and repeat. Carry on doing this until you find you can think a little more clearly.

Notice the season

12

Do you know what time of year it is not by the date but just through observation? Notice today where the leaves are in their life cycle: are they budding, creating a canopy of shade, or dropping? Your awareness will help you to see the overall picture in life, contributing to your general wisdom.

Which native flowers are in bloom? Does your mood echo the season in any way? It's common to experience a heightened sense of potential in Spring and of contemplation in Autumn. Today, begin to notice the links between your inner and outer environment.

13 Log your food

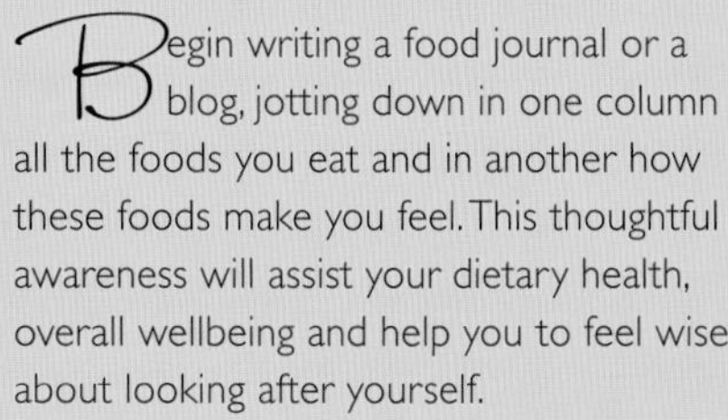

Begin writing a food journal or a blog, jotting down in one column all the foods you eat and in another how these foods make you feel. This thoughtful awareness will assist your dietary health, overall wellbeing and help you to feel wise about looking after yourself.

Be aware of any physical reactions you experience. This might include unpleasant feelings of being bloated or even having headaches. Consider emotional responses, too, such as guilt or pleasure.

Reasons to be wise

14

There are a zillion reasons why you should want to become more self-aware, savvy and wise. Take five minutes to brainstorm a few of these, thinking about your relationships, your home life, education, work, self-esteem and spiritual life.

Write down the thoughts that immediately spring to mind. Woolly categories need pinning down with real, attainable goals, so now try to attach a concrete intention to each reason. You might decide, for example, that in order to get on at work, you need to speak out more in meetings or avoid eating foods that make you sleepy during the afternoon. Think of these concrete goals as stepping stones to inner wisdom and pin them up to remind yourself of them throughout the day.

15 Start small

Instant wisdom

LEARN A NEW WORD

Open a dictionary and choose a random word. Learn its meaning and drop it into three conversations today.

What can you do today to bring your everyday life more in line with your intentions to be a wiser person? It's easiest to start small. You might decide to plant some seeds in potting compost, call the library to find out its opening hours or do an online search for local adult education classes.

If you have built castles in the air, your work need not be lost; that is where they should be. Now put the foundations under them.

Henry David Thoreau

Watch your breathing

16

To function at their optimum, the body and brain need a good supply of oxygen and adequate disposal of carbon dioxide. This will help your overall health and wellbeing as well as your inner wisdom.

If you inhale deeply and exhale fully, this is exactly what you get, but most of us don't. To check how efficiently you breathe, sit quietly and rest one palm on your upper chest and the other on your abdomen. Feel how they move when you breathe.

Your lower hand should rise when you take an in-breath and sink when you exhale. If your upper hand moves instead, you are breathing too shallowly. Practice this simple exercise often, focusing attention on your lower hand.

Just as much as we see in others we have in ourselves.

William Hazlitt

17 Try Mountain Pose

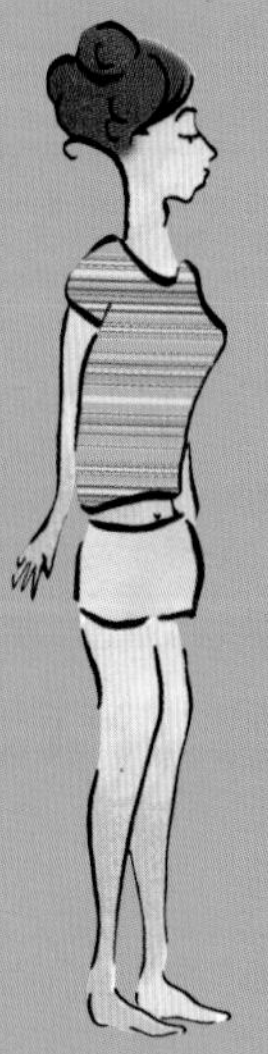

This yoga pose is the foundation of all standing postures and roots you so firmly to the earth that you are freed to extend up into the clouds.

Stand with feet together or a hip-width apart. Balance your weight evenly between both sides and the front and back of your feet. Lift your ankles, knees and thighs, broaden the backs of your thighs, drop your tailbone and feel how stable you are from the hips down. Relax your arms loosely by your sides. Now lengthen your spine, lift the breastbone, broaden your chest, drop your shoulders and lengthen the back of your neck. Hold this pose for 30–60 seconds, breathing evenly.

Respect other people

18

On your journey through the day, notice how other people behave to each other and to you. A big part of being a wise person is treating others with respect and generosity.

Do you notice any bad habits you share with other people, such as putting down achievements or not allowing others to finish sentences? Which traits do you admire in others and which could you emulate yourself? How might you stop yourself behaving so insensitively?

You might, for instance, try to act like the co-worker who offers encouraging words of praise, or like the mother who crouches down to reason with a bored toddler.

19 Move wisely

How you move reveals a great deal about your personality and shows how well you control your circumstances and emotions. Physical self-control is all part of being a wise person.

Watch how you routinely open a door. Do you grab the handle and tug, twisting your body and using more force than necessary?

Now consciously practice this action with poise and grace. Lift only your forearm, bending at the elbow. Don't hunch your shoulders or tense your jaw. Clasp the handle lightly, as if beginning to shake hands, then turn your wrist, without moving your upper arm or body. Let go before walking through the doorway. Practice using minimal force in other everyday movements.

Change your outlook

20

When you notice something wrong in the world today, don't be the person who looks in the other direction or moans to others. A wise person tries to be the one who has the chutzpah and insight to start making changes.

If you see injustice in the world of politics or international relations why not join an organization to add your name to those campaigning for change?

If you feel like starting with something closer to home, for example if something is broken at work, from the coffee machine to the photocopier, make it your responsibility to find out who to speak to (and hassle) to get it fixed.

You must be the change you wish to see in the world.

Mahatma Gandhi

21 Try Corpse Pose

Man's mind, once stretched by a new idea, never regains its original dimensions.

Oliver Wendell Holmes

This pose replicates the total rest of death, leaving you renewed and ready to re-engage with the world. Cover up well to prevent your body temperature dropping, then lie on your back with your legs outstretched, feet apart and toes dropping outward. Rest your arms away from your sides, palms facing upward. Elongate the back of your neck and relax your eyes, jaw and mouth. Lie here for five to ten minutes without moving.

Imagine letting go of physical tension and mental stresses each time you take an out-breath. Visualize your body becoming heavier and feel your back and legs sinking into the floor. Finally, wriggle your fingers and toes, roll to one side, then the other, to rest before opening your eyes and carefully sitting up.

Work with your body

22

Homeopaths and other holistic health practitioners believe in the body's natural ability to rebalance itself. They refer to this natural capacity for maintaining equilibrium in body and mind as 'homeostasis'. This innate body wisdom is thrown out of balance by physical and mental stress, lack of exercise, lack of sleep and not enough healthy foods.

Nurture your capacity for self-renewal by looking after your body and mind; by eating well, getting plenty of exercise and rest and by coping with stress in a positive way.

Wise thought

EAT FRESH FOODS

Try to eat mostly unprocessed foods by filling your basket from the fresh produce, fish and meat counters.

23 Think about your roots

What are your core values? These are the basics that will keep you grounded as you explore the many paths to greater wisdom.

Try to write your values down. If you can't put words to your values, think about which beliefs you would carry forward from your own childhood to share with a child growing up today. Perhaps you could pinpoint a belief in the innate goodness of others or the importance of education. Write these down. Then think about which aspects of your childhood you would transform, such as your relationships with your brothers and sisters. Write these down, too.

Do something different

24

Surprise yourself today by responding to life in a new way and see how invigorated it makes you feel. This can help you to become more thoughtful, insightful and wise.

Do you usually keep your head down and your thoughts to yourself? Try cracking a joke or sharing a story about your past. Or, if you want to try something really different, why not try gardening by the moon's cycles (research 'biodynamic gardening')? It's a truly spiritual experience.

25 Energize your base chakra

In yogic thought, the energy center deep within the pelvic region relates to who you are at your core; where you belong and how secure you feel about this.

To develop your sense of stability, self-understanding and ability to feel at home in your skin, sit quietly and visualize this area of the body flooded with warm, red light.

Call your family

26

When was the last time you called your siblings or parents? These are the people who knew you in your formative years and understand the forces that forged your personality and lifestyle. Try to draw on that insight, even if it seems irrelevant or you cast it aside long ago.

Play more often

27

Invite friends over to play board games, charades or 'hunt the thimble'. Living wiser is not about trying to be cool, but feeling liberated and self-confident enough to revel in the creative, life-affirming properties of silliness and fun.

28 Who helped mold you?

Make a list of all the people who helped to mold your character during your formative years and who were not part of your immediate family. The list probably includes teachers, neighbors, childhood friends and your peers at school. Today, think about which of your good qualities you owe to these people. And how difficult encounters made you a more astute, shrewd or wise individual.

Wind down well

29

Disengage your brain from all your work thoughts and to-do lists by winding down well in the evening.

Begin a couple of hours before bedtime by engaging in repetitive, untaxing tasks, such as tidying or washing dishes, then relax in a warm bath and enjoy a calming read (but no thrillers!) or listen to music with between 60 and 80 beats per minute, which has been shown to induce sleep.

No man is an island, entire of itself; every man is a piece of the continent, a part of the main...

John Donne

30 Go to bed earlier

Instant wisdom

BEDROOM CALM

Make your bedroom a calm haven where body, mind and brain can relax. Move stimulants such as phones, laptops and TVs to more 'active' parts of the home.

Lack of sleep impairs our ability to process information and act wisely and efficiently on it. The average adult needs between seven and eight hours of sleep each night to function well, says the National Sleep Foundation.

However, you will need more than this if you are paying off a sleep 'debt'. So this evening try to get to bed earlier than usual, especially if you habitually sleep for less than seven hours per night.

Wise tale: the tree of life

31

A boy and an apple tree were friends and spent many long, happy days together. As the boy grew, he didn't visit the tree so often. The tree asked why. 'I need toys instead,' said the boy. 'Can you help?' The tree donated apples. The boy grew into a man. 'Why do you no longer visit?' asked the tree. 'I have a family now; can you help?' The tree offered his branches to build a house. The man retired. 'Why do you no longer visit?' asked the tree. 'I must see the world before I die,' said the man. 'Can you help?' The tree gave his trunk as a boat. Finally, the man returned to the withered roots. 'I have nothing left to give,' said the tree. 'I only need somewhere to rest,' replied the man, and settled against the roots. The tree was happy.

Wisdom: *you are the man and the tree is your parents.*

checklist 1 How did you do?

Whether you tried out several ideas this month or just one, you might like to reflect on what you chose to try and why, and if it worked for you.

1. How many activities did you try this month?

- 1–3 activities ☐
- 4–10 activities ☐
- 11–20 activities ☐
- 21–31 activities ☐

2. How many did you repeat several times in the month?

- 1–3 activities ☐
- 4–10 activities ☐
- 11–20 activities ☐
- 21–31 activities ☐

3. Which activities had a positive effect on your sense of innate wisdom this month?

Use the page opposite to make notes about what worked for you and what didn't.

Notes, jottings and thoughts

32 Write with awareness

Take something from the Zen artist into your own expressive life. Have ready a paper and a calligraphy pen or a brush loaded with paint. Exhale fully, take a deep breath in, then, as you exhale slowly and steadily, draw a line.

Put all your attention into the act; just bat away other thoughts. Repeat as many times as you like. Can you understand how that line expresses the true you inside?

The infinite is in the finite of every instant.

Zen saying

Breakfast for the mind

33

Help to fortify your brain by eating a good breakfast every day, because studies suggest that people who do so tend to have enhanced concentration and perform better at work and school; all leading to the formation of a wise person.

Good food choices to boost your mental acuity include porridge, eggs, wholemeal toast, pancakes and fruit.

34 Brainstorm 'yourself'

Instant wisdom

SET DEADLINES

Give yourself 50 minutes to complete a certain task, then take a ten-minute breather before returning to it once again. You'll feel refreshed and reinspired.

Try out this exercise to help you explore yourself and find out how you tick. This will help you to discover the wiser you.

Make a personal 'mind map'. Sit down with a blank sheet of paper and write 'me' in the center of it. Draw lines branching out from the word and at the end of each one write a word that you connect with yourself.

These words could describe your attributes and personality traits, likes and dislikes, both good and bad qualities, people and places that have influenced you. Add to it during the day until you have a well-balanced word portrait of yourself, which will help your self-knowledge no end.

Looking again

35

Being perceptive is a simple activity. Almost as simple as checking back over your work to spot omissions and errors. Today, double-check every word you type or job you complete for errors. Don't blame yourself about any mistakes you make, since to be human is to err; simply notice patterns in the way you do things and think about how you might prevent mistakes in future.

Is there something in your makeup that makes you slap-dash or so eager to progress to the next stage that you neglect the finer details? Ponder this wise thought as you enquire within.

36 Yoga for change

Change means softening yourself rather than becoming brittle or hard in the face of self-reflection or implied criticism. This will help you build up your inner wisdom. Yoga can help you with this.

When you feel vulnerable, sit on your heels and bend forward, resting your chest on your thighs (or a firm cushion) and your forehead on the floor (or another cushion). Place your hands beside your feet. As you breathe out, let the difficult thoughts go and feel your chest relax and your upper back and neck soften. Enjoy the soothing pressure on your belly as you breathe in.

We must always change, renew, rejuvenate ourselves; otherwise we harden.

Goethe

Try Dandasana Pose

37

The Dandasana Pose in yoga is the foundation of many of the well-known sitting poses, stimulating the vital energy store in the central core of your body. This will set you up for a productive day in which your inner wisdom can come to the fore.

Sit with your legs outstretched and together. Stretch the backs of your knees down and bend your toes toward you. Place your palms beside your hips and press down. Then lift your trunk out of your hips, lengthening your sides and spine. Broaden your chest, lift your breastbone and align and extend the back of your neck. Hold this for 30 seconds, pushing into your heels.

38 Open your ears

On your journey to work, try this listening awareness exercise because developing your awareness is all part of the growth of inner wisdom.

Choose a sound near you, such as the rustle of a newspaper or someone talking. Listen intently to the sound (not the words). Notice its tone, rhythm and cadences, stops and starts. Now find a sound in the mid-distance, perhaps the rush of traffic. Listen intently again. Now try to find a sound much further away, such as a plane or birdsong. Try to tune your ear into its qualities, excluding all other noises from your soundscape.

Work that journal

39

People who seem wise tend to be highly organized and the secret to an organized mind is writing things down so that they are 'outside' your head. Keeping a journal is effective for this; think of it as your portable memory stick. Missed business appointments and forgotten birthdays can now be a thing of the past.

Choose a journal with whole-day entries, or even with times of the day included. Start every Monday morning by looking at the week ahead, filling in appointments, deadlines, birthdays and dates. Note calls you need to make and people you need to talk to. At the end of each day, strike out tasks you have achieved and write down how much time each one took (to aid future time-management). Move unfinished tasks to a new day. Start each day by consulting your journal.

Wise thought

BE CONFIDENT

If you don't think you'll remember something, you are more likely to forget it.

40 Morning tune-in

Before crawling out of bed this morning, spend a couple of minutes getting wised up on any messages your body has for you. Is any particular area stiff? Which stretches might help you? Your body instinctively knows this, so follow its prompts. Which parts already feel great? Tune in to that innate vitality.

41 Read new news

Where the eyes and ears go, the brain follows.

Indian saying

Try out a new newspaper this morning, or buy one, if it's not one of your regular habits. Gaining a change of perspective on local issues and your place in global events kickstarts the brain and challenges lazy assumptions.

Read then act

42

Since the era of the Romantic poets in the late 18th century, writers have urged us to get out for ourselves and experience the enlightenment that occurs quite naturally when we spend time in wild settings. This form of wisdom is often described as a sense of great peace. The overwhelming sense of identification with the natural world can bring fresh insight into the human condition.

Climb the mountains and get their good tidings. Nature's peace will flow into you as sunshine flows into trees. The winds will blow their freshness into you, and the storms their energy, while cares will drop off like autumn leaves.

John Muir

43

Visualize your spine

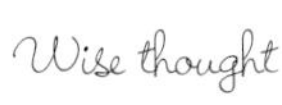

STRIKING A BALANCE

Alternate periods of study with physical activity. This seems to 'fix' facts into the memory.

Close your eyes and sit up straight with your feet flat on the floor. Can you sense your spine? This vital body part is your center and lies at the root of your body wisdom. It is also the seat of your intelligence, for located in the spinal canal are nerves that communicate with every other body part.

Feel the back of your spine facing the world behind you, then think about the front of your spine facing forward. Try to lift your spine today, so that the front and back lengthen equally.

Ball park/retail park?

46

Leisure time is important and adds to the learning that results in wisdom. When you have an odd moment today, do a mental audit of where you tend to spend most of your leisure time. If your answer is shopping malls and supermarkets, maybe it's time to brainstorm wiser, more rewarding, ways to spend your precious hours (and cash). Think of places you could indulge your loves and your lusts; maybe at the skating rink, theater or in a real park.

47 Gaze at the night sky

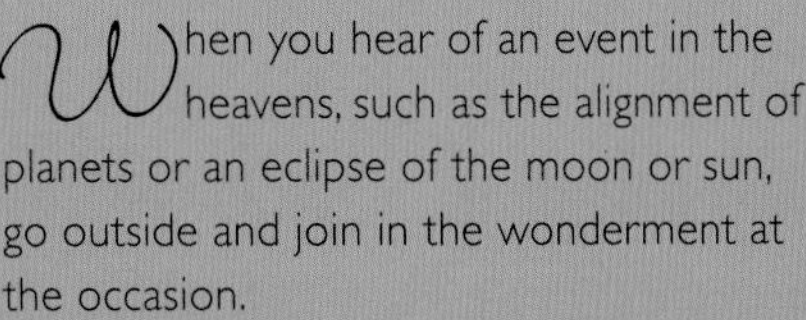

When you hear of an event in the heavens, such as the alignment of planets or an eclipse of the moon or sun, go outside and join in the wonderment at the occasion.

As you look up, feel a sense of our place in the universe. Use the moment as a spur to add to your knowledge and find out more about our galaxy, the history of the stars and their movement across the night sky. Do you know where the moon comes up tonight, and where it goes down?

Work out your workout

48

Have you taken enough exercise today to keep your brain alert and allow your body to tell you how amazing it can feel? Most days we need at least 30 minutes of physical activity that leaves us slightly out of breath.

Get your journal out this morning and write in at least three sessions over the next week. They don't have to be in the gym; brisk walking is fantastic exercise, as is using a lawnmower, clipping a hedge by hand, mopping a floor or changing bed linen.

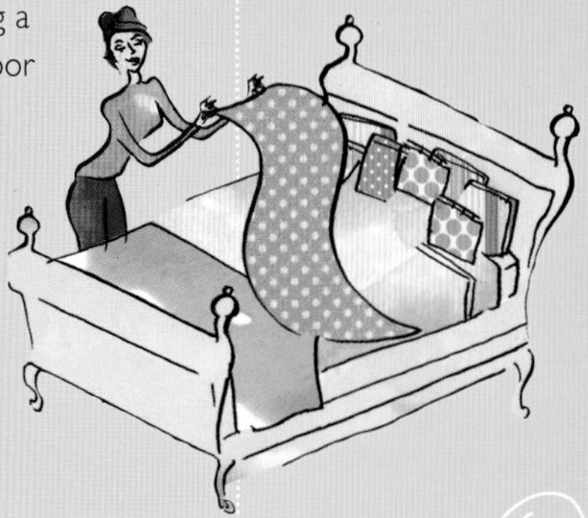

49 Turn off the TV

Wise thought

ASK A FRIEND
If you find it hard to stop watching the TV, ask a friend to look after your remote for one day a week.

If you do only one thing to learn more about your complex inner life, turn off the TV set. You will find that this instantly frees up time to spend on more edifying entertainment, such as listening to music, reading or conversation, and it frees your body from the confines of the sofa. Try bread-making or planting seeds for relaxing activities that stimulate the body as well as the imagination.

Sit with spirit

50

On your way home tonight, stop to sit in a place that has a history of spiritual meaning to others. It could be a chapel, cathedral or temple, a holy well or a special tree.

Just sit. Close your eyes. Can you feel the sense of serenity yet liveliness brought about by years of worship, ritual and prayer? Enjoy it without thinking too deeply about it.

51 Words of wisdom

The great 13th-century Japanese Zen Buddhist teacher Dogen explained that spiritual practice, in his case sitting for meditation known as 'zazen', was not just a way to enlightenment, it *was* enlightenment. Even for beginners. If you live a spiritual life, don't trouble yourself about getting to the much-mythologized world of wisdom; you are already there, as long as you continue that practice.

To study the self is to forget the self.
To forget the self is to be enlightened by the ten thousand things.

Dogen Zenji

Investigate a great life

52

If you can decide to do without your TV for a while, use your TV-free hours to become better informed about someone who has changed the way we live and view the world. It might be a scientist, such as Isaac Newton or Charles Darwin, a voice of compassion, such as the Dalai Lama, or someone who has fought to make society a more just place, such as Martin Luther King Jnr. All these individuals can impart their wisdom to you, in their different ways.

Instant wisdom

LEARN FROM OTHER LIVES

Read a biography of one of the great figures from history and immerse yourself in the detail of their lives.

53 Explore calligraphy

Instant wisdom

ZEN INSPIRATION
Hang a piece of Zen calligraphy above the place where you sit and relax, to enlighten both yourself and all those who come to visit.

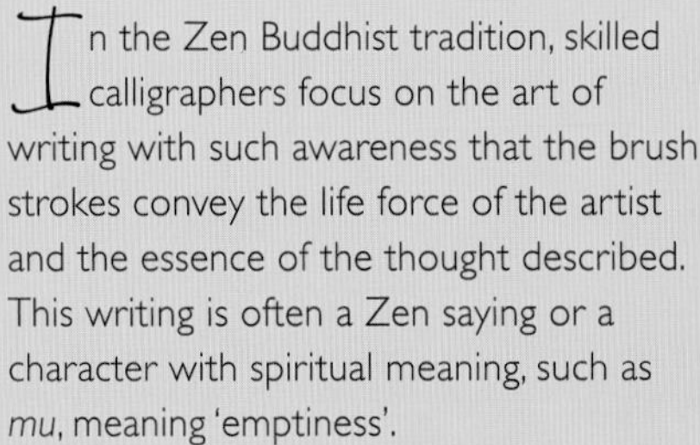

In the Zen Buddhist tradition, skilled calligraphers focus on the art of writing with such awareness that the brush strokes convey the life force of the artist and the essence of the thought described. This writing is often a Zen saying or a character with spiritual meaning, such as *mu*, meaning 'emptiness'.

The artist sets out with a blank canvas and a mind made empty of emotions, thoughts and expectation by meditation. In this state, the act of expressing the idea is so full of vitality, purity and depth that it draws the mind of the viewer toward enlightenment.

Why not try exploring calligraphy? Use a beginner's set of equipment, including brush, ink, rice paper and a how-to guide.

Find mental space

54

Today, let's tackle some brain clutter. Sit quietly, close your eyes and watch your breath moving in and out. You won't be able to stem the tide of thoughts that ebb and flow, but what you can do is look for the spaces between the thoughts. Rest in the pauses whenever you can.

Our life is frittered away by detail. Simplify, simplify.

Henry David Thoreau

Open a window

55

When your brain is befuddled and you can't think straight, open a window, stick your head out and take three deep breaths in and out. Even in the city, the refreshing properties of outdoor air are a mind tonic.

56 Lemon balm bath

Lemon balm is valued by herbalists for waking the brain and rebalancing the emotions. Start your day by placing a few dried lemon balm leaves in a teapot and pour over 500 ml (17 fl oz) of boiling water. Infuse for ten minutes while you run a bath. Sip a cup of the tea as you relax in the bath and pour the remaining tea into it, inhaling its scent in the steam.

Balm is sovereign for the brain, strengthening the memory and powerfully chasing away melancholy.

John Evelyn

Take a woodland walk

57

Studies show that spending time in woodland is good for your mental health and wisdom in general, and that it is especially beneficial for children.

Find out today where your nearest wood or wilderness is and plan a trip there. Take a picnic and a tree-identification guide. Can you find and identify leaves from five different trees?

58 Deeper reflection

The sensory thrills of the world as experienced through the media are fantastically attractive. But just for tonight put them aside by turning off the TV and your computer. Switch off your phone, too.

Now simply sit quietly and imagine looking inside, toward your heart. Here, deep within yourself, is a source of beauty and satisfying sweetness that does not require electricity or money and is not founded on other people's dreams. Enjoy the journey of self-discovery and reflect on this thought.

Locate your inner genius

59

Each of us can do something inspired by the work and lives of a great person. What small act, conversation or task will you carry out or have today that was prompted by this person? The lives of others can give you inspiring ideas to help you find your own inner wisdom.

Everyone is a genius at least once a year. The real geniuses simply have their bright ideas closer together.

Georg Christoph Lichtenberg

60 Dance barefoot

Instant wisdom

SILENT DISCOS

Look for silent discos, where you can dance in public spaces with a mass of other people, all plugged into their own sounds, but coming together as one body.

Do something that makes you feel carefree today. The wise are able to rise above the cares of the world.

Dancing barefoot outdoors is often effective, since aerobic exercise stimulates the brain, calms anxiety and brings about a sensation of happiness. Find a good-sized piece of grass or sand, plug in your iPod, shake off your shoes and just dance.

Wise tale: Celtic cauldron

61

Long ago, according to Welsh legend, the enchantress Ceridwen, goddess of poetry and divine inspiration, brewed a cauldron of inspiration and science. The resulting mead would confer great wisdom, creative powers and knowledge of the future on whoever sipped it. Every day she gathered more charmed ingredients and magical herbs, which she simmered and stirred for a year and a day, until the potion was reduced to three blessed drops of knowledge. By chance they spilt onto the finger of a servant boy, who was instantly enlightened and became the visionary Welsh poet Taliesin.

Wisdom: *add ingredients day by day to your own cauldron of wisdom, allowing them to bubble and condense so thoroughly that your understanding transforms the lives of those around you, whether you intend it or not.*

checklist 2 How did you do?

Whether you tried out several ideas this month or just one, you might like to reflect on what you chose to try and why, and if it worked for you.

1. How many activities did you try this month?

- 1–3 activities ☐
- 4–10 activities ☐
- 11–20 activities ☐
- 21–30 activities ☐

2. How many did you repeat several times in the month?

- 1–3 activities ☐
- 4–10 activities ☐
- 11–20 activities ☐
- 21–30 activities ☐

3. Which activities had a positive effect on your sense of innate wisdom this month?

Use the page opposite to make notes about what worked for you and what didn't.

Notes, jottings and thoughts

62 Wake up earlier

If you find it tricky to make time for morning meditation, set your alarm to ring 15 minutes earlier than usual.

Just 15 minutes of meditation is enough to tune in to your inner wisdom, starting the day as you mean to go on. After a week or so, set your alarm another 15 minutes earlier to gain a daily 30-minute slot.

Standing Leg Lift

63

Yogis say that our inner wisdom is located at the base of the spine and lies dormant until awakened. Begin this process by increasing flexibility in the pelvis, toning the spine and boosting circulation in the legs.

Stand tall with your feet hip-width apart and facing forward. Lift one leg and rest the heel on a low wall or stool. Straighten the leg, lift up through your standing leg and raise your arms overhead in front of you. Hold this for 30 seconds. Repeat on the other leg.

64 Look within

Sit in a meditative position this morning and begin your practice simply by watching your breath. After a few minutes, when you feel calm and your breathing has become smooth and deep, ask yourself these two simple questions: 'What do I most desire?' and 'What stops me from reaching it?' Don't rack your brain for answers; let them emerge. If it is helpful, ponder the following quotation:

What more do you want, O soul! And what else do you search for outside, when within yourself you possess your riches, delights, satisfactions, fullness, and kingdom – your Beloved whom you desire and seek?

St John of the Cross

Start a dream journal

65

The unconscious mind operates at a deeper level than our everyday consciousness and has many wise messages for us, and often delivers them cryptically, in the form of dreams.

Keep a notebook and pen beside your bed. On waking, jot down what you remember of your dreams. You don't have to write complete sentences and your jottings don't need to make sense; just try to get down the images and feelings they evoke.

Wise thought

CHECK WHAT YOU WRITE

Read over everything you write for errors, and check unfamiliar words or names in a dictionary.

66

Be money-wise

Live within your means is the mantra of the money-wise. To find out how much money comes in and goes out of your accounts each month, sit down this evening and take a close look at all your bank and credit-card statements.

List all incoming money in one column. In another column, list all your outgoings: spending on housing, tax, pension, lighting, heating, phone, transport and food. Do the two figures tally? Why not? Working this out is the first step toward living wisely within your means.

Get on your bike

67

People who commute to work or school by bicycle tend to arrive feeling rejuvenated, awake and ready to go, thanks to the healthy dose of cardiovascular exercise. Because cyclists don't face gridlock, lack of parking spaces or train cancellations, they also arrive with an increased sense of independence and spontaneity, which can boost work relationships and performance. All these reasons make cycling the wisest travel option.

Wise thought

BIKE HEALTH

Be sure to have your bike serviced by a certified cycle-repair technician if you haven't used it for a while.

68 How are you seen?

Look at photos of yourself posted on social networking sites. Who do you see and what signals are you sending to the world? Do they really convey who you are or are they more about how you think you would like to be seen? Do they reflect the wiser you? Think about how a prospective employer might react to them. Do you need to change anything?

It is as hard to see one's self as to look backwards without turning around.

Henry David Thoreau

Watch your breath

69

Begin this morning by tuning in to your breath, which brings you back to the essence of who you are.

Sit comfortably with your spine upright and relax your shoulders and jaw. Close your eyes and gently seal your lips, breathing in and out through your nostrils. Now just watch your breathing, without trying to change it in any way. Notice how warm the out-breath is on your nostrils and how cooling the flow of breath in through your nose. Feel how your belly swells as you inhale and how your navel draws toward your spine as you exhale. Sense your ribs expanding to the side and backward. This still, calm person is the real you, and is there whenever you need her.

70 Stop crossing your legs

To keep your brain alert, feed it with plenty of freshly oxygenated blood. If you cross your legs, you are more likely to hunch forward and crunch your shoulders toward your ears. These restrictions prevent the free flow of blood around the body and up to the seat of wisdom, the brain.

71 Book an eye test

When was the last time you had your eyes tested? If it was more than two years ago, book an appointment today. Wisdom means using your eyes well, which becomes effortless if you have glasses with a correct prescription, if you need them.

Take a scent break

72

The brain needs regular breaks from work. Keep Eau de Cologne in your purse for a quick scent meditation. Spray it on a tissue and hold it to your nose.

Can you discern the scent's top note? What is the heady first impression? Describe it in words. Then 'listen' for the middle notes; the more rounded impressions at the heart of a fragrance. Again, try to describe them. Finally, pick out all the rich base notes; those that linger. Can you identify any single ingredients, such as rosemary, lemon or lavender?

Instant wisdom

JOG YOUR MEMORY

Switch on your senses when taking in information: touch, smell and taste, if you can, to promote memory retention.

73 Use lists

Instant wisdom

TO DO

Carry to-do lists in your journal or electronically so that they are always at your fingertips.

To help to stimulate your short-term memory, practice the art of list-making. Why not start a three-list system? You can create one list for immediate must-dos, one for jobs to complete this week and one for long-term tasks. At the end of the day, strike off items you have achieved and shuffle tasks between the lists.

At the end of each week, check that entries on the long-term list are progressing. If something stays on your daily list for more than three days, try to think about why this might be so.

Say hello to prudence

74

Do you know what the word 'prudence' means? How could you apply this principle to your financial affairs and how might it affect your work life or your personal relationships? How might it contribute to your overall wisdom?

Prudence is the knowledge of things to be sought, and those to be shunned.

Marcus Tullius Cicero

75 Taste freedom

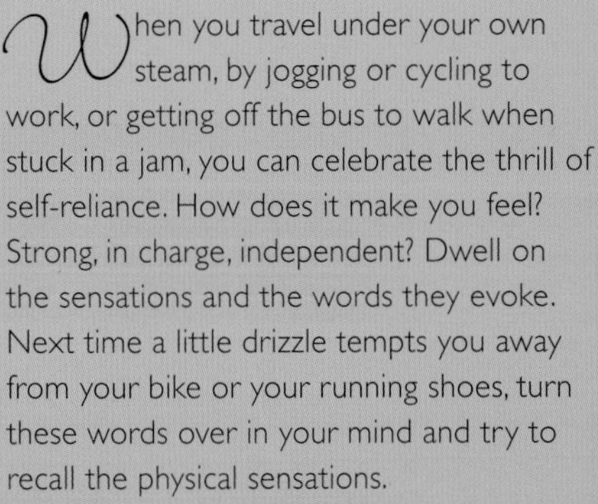

When you travel under your own steam, by jogging or cycling to work, or getting off the bus to walk when stuck in a jam, you can celebrate the thrill of self-reliance. How does it make you feel? Strong, in charge, independent? Dwell on the sensations and the words they evoke. Next time a little drizzle tempts you away from your bike or your running shoes, turn these words over in your mind and try to recall the physical sensations.

When once you have tasted flight, you will forever walk the earth with your eyes turned skyward, for there you have been, and there you will always long to return.

Henry Van Dyke

Clear out your closet

76

Our closets tend to harbor thoughts that prevent us from stepping forward into a wiser future. Take everything you own out of your closet and have the courage today to pass on or throw away garments that remind you of unhappy relationships, that no longer fit, or that keep you anchored to previous decades or lifestyles. Rehang only those clothes that make you feel capable, sage, smart or sassy.

77

Don't use your camera

Next time you visit somewhere special, record your visit with a sketchbook and pencil rather than a camera. This forces you to stay still in one place, to fully observe detail, texture, light and shadow. All this sensual engagement with a place not only draws to the surface vital reserves of energy and creativity from deep within, it roots you to a place, making a special connection for the future. A camera places a screen between you and the experience and two screens when looked at in an online photo album.

Mere color, unspoiled by meaning and unallied with definite form, can speak to the soul in a thousand different ways.

Oscar Wilde

Put those magazines back

78

Celebrity magazines aren't very helpful on the journey to greater wisdom. The assumptions on which they are built tend to foster unkind emotions, such as avarice, envy, delight in failure and prying.

A study reported that every women who looked at images of skinny, glamorous women in magazines felt depressed about their body image, no matter how svelte or glamorous they actually were themselves. Challenge yourself to stop buying magazines, or only to indulge in them when you visit the hairdresser or beauty salon.

79 Assess your diet

Instant wisdom

CLEAR THINKING
Carry an apple and a bag of mixed nuts in your purse to maintain your ability to think straight throughout the day.

If you have been keeping a food journal, look back at it. Now you are this far into your journey, you should be able to spot patterns emerging. Try to pinpoint which foods leave you feeling clear-headed and buzzing with energy. Put these items at the top of your shopping list or online supermarket order.

If you would like to become better informed about why we tend to eat foods that don't make us feel this good, try these books, which are a good read as well as full of fascinating food facts: *Eat Your Heart Out* by Felicity Lawrence and *Animal, Vegetable, Miracle* by Barbara Kingsolver.

Safeguard your eyes

80

To preserve your powers of visual perception (the wise are renowned for their acute eyesight) always be sure to wear sunglasses in bright sunlight (Winter as well as Summer). The best protection comes from lenses made to block 100 per cent of ultraviolet radiation: UVA, UVB and UVC rays. Excessive exposure to these rays can lead to degenerative eye conditions including age-related macular degeneration. If you work outdoors, wrap-around shades and a wide-brimmed hat will offer you the best protection.

Men in general judge more by the sense of sight than by the sense of touch, because everyone can see, but only a few can test by feeling.

Niccolò Machiavelli

81 Be generous of heart

If, from force of habit, you catch yourself reaching out for a celebrity magazine or clicking through to a gossip site, try to check yourself.

For a moment, think about how it will make you feel. After the initial thrill, do you feel generous of heart, kind, compassionate? Probably not. But these qualities, said The Buddha, are the ones that make our world a better place. What reading matter would stimulate those feelings in you and provoke you to act on them?

Teach this triple truth to all: a generous heart, kind speech, and a life of service and compassion are the things which renew humanity.

The Buddha

Treat yourself

82

When the journey seems daunting and you stumble, keep faith by making things easier for yourself.

Do something that raises your spirits today and every day; whatever makes you feel really good about yourself. Maybe this could include anything from putting on lipstick or beautiful shoes to soaking in a hot tub or going for a run on the beach.

83 Picture a tortoise

Wisdom is something you acquire slowly and gradually. To remind yourself of this, why not keep an image of a tortoise as your screensaver or as a fridge magnet? In many Japanese monasteries, a tortoise is kept as a pet; a tangible reminder that seeking the truth requires slow, steady attention and perseverance. In folk tales from around the globe, from Aesop's fables to India's *Panchatantra*, it is the tortoise who wins the race in the end.

Taking the smallest step forward or change for the good, many religions teach, starts to change the world, and a moment's good deeds affects the rest of time.

Paint your front door

84

As the transition point between your private and public worlds, the front door of your home shows everyone what you think of yourself and the pride that you take in yourself.

Demonstrate this by giving your front door a new coat of paint and placing a couple of plants in pots on either side. In India, this is thought to draw energy and positivity into your life. Spending time at your door has the added benefit of bringing you into contact with neighbors. The world becomes a wiser, more connected, place if we engage with our community.

85 After-exercise tune-in

Never does nature say one thing and wisdom another.
Juvenal

After cooling down from a morning run, exercise class or gym session, lie on your back with your knees bent and feet flat on the floor. You'll find that you'll benefit from your exercise that much more.

Rest your arms by your side or place your palms on your abdomen. Close your eyes and look inside your body. Enjoy the post-exercise sensations. Take your attention, in turn, to your head, your hands and feet, the large muscles in your legs and arms and to your mind. Try to capture these fantastic feelings so that you can motivate future exercise sessions.

Thought for today

86

Today, spend at least 30 minutes on an activity that leaves you feeling calm and centered. It might be a walk along the cliffs, capturing a scene in watercolors, solving a particularly intricate jigsaw puzzle or volunteering to work in a soup kitchen. Once you feel calm, close your eyes and sense the stillness and wisdom at your core. Then think about these wise words:

That which is the finest essence – this whole world has that as its soul. That is Reality. That is the Self. That art thou.

Chandogya Upanishad 6.8.7

87 List your needs

If you experienced a stressful patch today, think about how you coped with it. Did you rage or tie yourself in knots? How might you have handled the situation more wisely?

Wisdom means facing the fact that life can be stressful and hectic and looking for ways to help you cope. Take five minutes to list some attainable options. Perhaps you could try improving the quality of your life by having a babysitter once every two weeks, or help with the house-cleaning, a regular hour on your own or a nurturing yoga class. Who could you ask to help you achieve this? Give them a call.

Cool your temper

88

A hot temper can prevent us from responding appropriately to flashpoints and only exacerbates problems. Today, when you feel your temperature rising, try the following strategies before expressing yourself in words or deeds.

First, breathe in for a count of four and out for a count of four; repeat three times. Second, think about your life in five years' time. Will today's flashpoint matter then? Finally, ask yourself what your calmest, best-balanced friend would do in this situation. If these techniques work for you, file them away for future use.

Instant wisdom

PRODUCTIVE ANGER

Anger can feel intoxicating because of the rush of chemicals you experience. Vent them productively by taking up kick-boxing or joining a debating society.

89 Unfinished business

Instant wisdom

COMPLETE TASKS
Finish one job before moving on to another.

Before this month ends, bring one unresolved issue from your past to light and list the ways you could begin to tackle it to bring you the peace of mind needed to move through this year's journey.

Ask yourself what you need to do, what help you require and who you need to talk to. Write those things down in a logical order and make a start on the first one today.

The block of granite which is an obstacle in the pathway of the weak, becomes a stepping-stone in the pathway of the strong.

Thomas Carlyle

Night lessons

90

Few of us choose to experience night. Tonight, once it is dark, sit in front of a window with the lights turned off, or, if you can, sit outdoors in a quiet, dark garden and look into the darkness. Think about the qualities of day such as sun, light, heat, action, clarity and vision. Now think about the qualities of night: shade, dark, coldness, introspection and obscurity. What can these qualities offer you on a journey to greater wisdom?

You might like to visualize or look at a yin-yang symbol. See how light and darkness define each other, forming a perfect whole. Notice how each one has the seed of its opposite within it. They are interdependent. To be truly wise, we must appreciate the eternal balance and constant movement between opposing forces and be open to the change this inevitably brings.

91 Walk by the moon

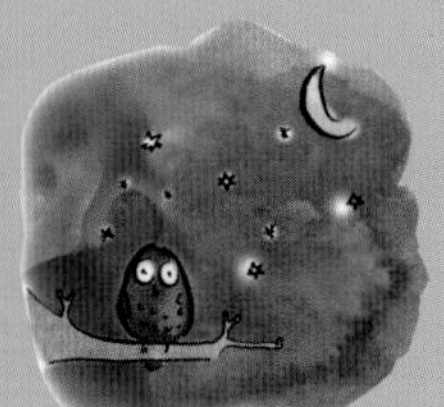

Walking in darkness, when your visual perception is reduced, amplifies your powers of hearing and sense of texture, which opens up the mind to new thoughts and innovative ways of looking at the world. Try it at full moon, taking a friend with you or going with a group of like-minded people. Try to walk in silence, better to appreciate the nightlife and all the sounds you make in a quiet landscape. When you arrive at your final destination, spend time lying on your back looking up at the sky.

If a man wishes to be sure of the road he treads on, he must close his eyes and walk in the dark.

St John of the Cross

Wise tale: Athena

92

From Ancient Greece comes the tale of the goddess Athena bathing naked in a pool. Tiresias, a shepherd's son, came upon her. To witness a well-known goddess without her heavenly coverings was a mortal sin, and this goddess was the ever-armed goddess of war, so he was terrified. However, the mighty warrior Athena is also goddess of wisdom, reason and judgment. Though she blinded Tiresias to this world by laying her hands over his eyes to conceal her naked body, she also opened his eyes to far-sightedness, gifting him with the power of prophecy.

Wisdom: *think before you act; you have the power to transform others' lives with your gifts, even your warlike powers, if you choose to.*

checklist 3 How did you do?

Whether you tried out several ideas this month or just one, you might like to reflect on what you chose to try and why, and if it worked for you.

1. How many activities did you try this month?

- 1–3 activities ☐
- 4–10 activities ☐
- 11–20 activities ☐
- 21–31 activities ☐

2. How many did you repeat several times in the month?

- 1–3 activities ☐
- 4–10 activities ☐
- 11–20 activities ☐
- 21–31 activities ☐

3. Which activities had a positive effect on your sense of innate wisdom this month?

Use the page opposite to make notes about what worked for you and what didn't.

Notes, jottings and thoughts

93 Switch off the sat-nav

Wise thought

DON'T MULTITASK
Multitasking slows down performance by making the brain less efficient at processing information.

Nurture your inbuilt navigation system by turning off electronic gadgets that stop you from thinking about where you are and where you need to get to. Engaging with landscapes and maps gives the brain a good spatial workout.

Also, take inspiration from migrating birds who fly south for a certain number of days at a specific time of year. This is not learnt knowledge, but instinctive wisdom. Think about whether you feel compelled to do anything twice a year.

Organize your purse

94

Go to work tomorrow with your purse as fresh and well organized as your wise intentions. People who are well-organized give the impression of being wise, even if they don't feel particularly learned!

Tonight, put aside 30 minutes and shake the contents of the purse you take to work onto a table. First clear out all the garbage. Next tackle the must-dos: transfer phone numbers, to-do lists and memory-jogging notes to your phone, notebook and journal. Then sort like with like. Zip makeup and perfume into a pouch; put store cards, travel cards and money in a wallet and pens in a pencil case. Consider whether you need a separate bag for sports kit, cycling gear or work files. Then give your purse a wipe and, once dry, file everything in order, using all pockets. Tomorrow will be a breeze.

95 Try Triangle Pose

Start this morning by looking at the world from another plane. It will give you great insight.

Stand with feet together, then jump your feet and arms wide apart. Turn your left foot in slightly and your right foot 90° to the right. Breathe in. Exhaling, extend your upper body to the right without moving your legs or hips. Imagine you have walls in front of and behind you, keeping you in line. Rest your lower hand on your shin or ankle and stretch your top arm upward. Look up at your thumb. Hold for 30 seconds, then, inhaling, lift your upper body back to center, turn your feet forward and repeat to the other side.

Points of view

96

It's a wise move to look at everyday life from unusual angles. Try to do this intellectually, too.

At a museum, why not follow the children's trail rather than reading the signs for adults? Or buy a foreign newspaper or tune into radio news from another part of the globe? Then think about this wise quotation:

Some things and some people have to be approached obliquely, at an angle.

André Gide

97 Watch your thoughts

Sit quietly with your eyes closed, perhaps after practicing yoga or a breathing exercise, and picture your mind as a large screen on which your thoughts are projected. Spend a minute or so watching the pictures and enjoying the show, but without engaging your judgment or becoming emotionally entwined in the soap-opera plots. Realizing that your thoughts are not 'you' leads to a more profound understanding of your nature.

Make fresh mint tea

98

If you have a mint plant growing in your garden or on your windowsill, you may have enough leaves to brew your own aromatic pick-me-up tea.

Pluck two or three sprigs from the top of the plant, place them in a mug and pour over just-boiled water. Leave to infuse for five minutes, then sip, sweetened with a little honey if you have a sweet tooth. Savor the mind-awakening scented steam as well as the delicious taste.

PREPARE WELL

Drink soothing peppermint tea if stressful thoughts about a big day ahead lead to digestive problems or a headache.

99 Circle your future

Look at the diagram (or 'mind map') you made about yourself (see page 44). Take two marker pens, one red and one green. Circle in red the traits, people or places you would like to have less of in your life. With the green pen circle those you would like to make more of in the future.

On a separate piece of paper write down five practical ways to start making things happen such as 'Browse the small ads for a new apartment', 'Call Grandma' or 'Spend lunchtime in the bookstore'.

Take outdoor breaks

100

Today, try to take an outdoor break from your workstation. Research shows that moving around and being active outdoors 'fixes' information in the mind and makes it more likely that you'll return to your work with reduced restlessness and higher levels of concentration.

Breaks also help to relieve anxiety related to work issues. A Swedish study found that those who exercise outdoors feel more restored than gym-users.

101 The road to enlightenment

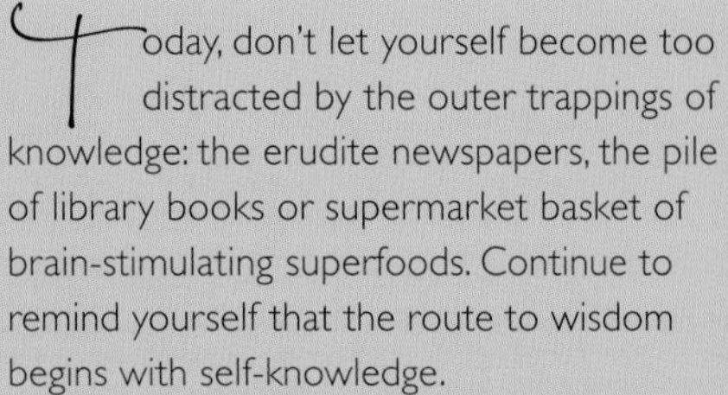

Today, don't let yourself become too distracted by the outer trappings of knowledge: the erudite newspapers, the pile of library books or supermarket basket of brain-stimulating superfoods. Continue to remind yourself that the route to wisdom begins with self-knowledge.

Write out the following quotation on a sticky note and fix it to your computer or to your bathroom mirror. What do you need to do to get to know your inner, wise person even better?

He who knows others is wise.
He who knows himself is enlightened.

Tao Te Ching

Eat healthy fats

102

Get a fix of brain-boosting fats this lunchtime by choosing small oily fish such as salmon, sardines and mackerel, or by drizzling your salad with olive oil. Oil also helps your body to access fat-soluble vitamins such as vitamin A, vital for eye health, and antioxidant vitamin E, which protects cell membranes from damage.

Morning thought

103

On waking this morning, reassure yourself that every new day offers another chance to start living more wisely and finding the real you, which is pure, happy and free. Pledge to yourself that you will meet whatever comes your way today with equanimity.

104 Snacks for wisdom

Wise thought

QUIT TODAY
Give up smoking; it lowers the IQ and your ability to think and be a wise person.

If you miss your breakfast or lunch you are likely to experience a marked slump in concentration and mental acuity mid-morning or mid-afternoon.

Instead of reaching for a packet of cookies or a bar of chocolate, which will send your blood-sugar levels and mood soaring and then crashing, try these easy-to-assemble snacks. They all contain foods shown to aid cognitive function: peanut butter and banana on a rice cake; muesli with milk and a handful of blueberries; oat crackers topped with avocado; or hummus with a selection sliced raw vegetables.

Sit and watch

105

Sit outdoors this lunchtime on a park bench and just spend some time watching the world going by.

Think about how the following haiku poem captures the 'is-ness' of the world in a cinematic present tense. Can you make up a string of words that also captures a sense of moments passing?

Old pond – frogs jumped in –
sound of water.

Matsuo Basho

Instant wisdom

EXPLAIN SUCCINCTLY
To get a grip on complex topics, try explaining them in a nutshell to other people.

106 Walking meditation

As you stride out during a work break today, see how it feels to coordinate your breath with your pace. Once you are into a rhythm with your walking, breathe in for two or three paces and out for two or three paces, whichever count you feel comfortable with.

Every time your mind starts to follow a train of thought, bring it back to your pace and the number. If you feel totally comfortable, lengthen the count so that your in- and out-breaths are extended, but always try to keep them equal.

After a day's walk everything has twice its usual value.

George Macauley Trevelyan

Moving river visualization

107

When something doesn't go quite according to plan today, use this exercise to wash away anxiety, control, guilt and blame.

Sit comfortably and close your eyes or look at a picture of a stream. Imagine you are sitting on the bank of a fast-flowing river or beside a waterfall. Hear the rush of water and the wind in the rushes. Now see yourself picking up dead leaves from the bank. Feel how dry and lifeless they are. Each one is a worry or a regret that serves no purpose.

One by one, hold the leaves over the moving water and let them go. Watch the leaves float off, borne away on the current of fresh water. Wriggle your fingers and toes before carefully opening your eyes.

Wise thought

A REAL STREAM

The exercise on this page is even more effective if you can find a real stream to sit beside.

108 Shine your mind

Today, try to approach the world around you with a sense of wonder, seeing the good in everything.

Think of your eyes as a torch, shining a light onto ordinary objects and illuminating their special quality, such as the determination of the weed pushing its way through concrete or the beauty of a city puddle's oily sheen.

To the dull mind all nature is leaden. To the illumined mind the whole world sparkles with light.

Ralph Waldo Emerson

Try aerobic exercise

109

Studies suggest that aerobic exercise seems to slow the decline of mental faculties such as memory, concentration and the ability to multitask as we age.

So make aerobic exercise part of your daily routine. Try it after work today and build it up to three hours a week to increase your total of brain neurons and their connections with each other. As well as brisk walking, try swimming, dance or exercise classes.

Wise thought

REVISION HINT

If you have an exam or interview the next day, stop revising in the afternoon and take some exercise, eat a healthy meal and get an early night.

110 Dealing with failure

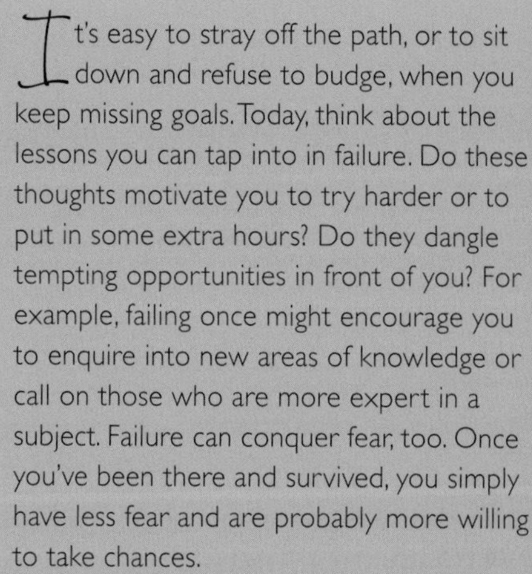

It's easy to stray off the path, or to sit down and refuse to budge, when you keep missing goals. Today, think about the lessons you can tap into in failure. Do these thoughts motivate you to try harder or to put in some extra hours? Do they dangle tempting opportunities in front of you? For example, failing once might encourage you to enquire into new areas of knowledge or call on those who are more expert in a subject. Failure can conquer fear, too. Once you've been there and survived, you simply have less fear and are probably more willing to take chances.

It is a mistake to suppose that men succeed though success; they much oftener succeed through failures.

Samuel Smiles

Cook from scratch

111

This morning, find a recipe that sounds delicious and do-able and make a list of ingredients. The sense of satisfaction and creativity will add to your personal stock of wisdom. Go shopping at lunchtime so you are well prepared to cook from scratch this evening. Fewer of us prepare food using raw ingredients than in the past, and in doing so we are neglecting to pass on key skills and soul-nurturing food wisdom to future generations.

As you cook, enjoy the feeling of skill and judgment that comes from creating something. Once you have mastered the dish, try to repeat it next week without looking at the recipe. This helps to fix it into your brain. Add a new dish to your repertoire at least once every two weeks.

112 Be an intelligent shopper

Your body knows instinctively which are the wisest food choices for you. But the signals get disrupted if you shop while you are hungry. You are very likely to buy way too much food and possibly the wrong type. To be an intelligent shopper, use a list or order online.

Tell me what you eat, I'll tell you who you are.

Jean Anthelme Brillat-Savarin

Join a library

113

If you wish to become more erudite, there is no better setting than a library. It's filled with wise thoughts and is free. Join a library near your workplace or home today and take out three books on subjects that intrigue you. Make one of those books an unusual choice for you. If you like literary fiction, for instance, choose a detective novel or a thriller by Stephen King. Start reading in bed tonight.

Wise thought

ASK A LIBRARIAN
Librarians are a font of knowledge. Tap into them by asking for recommendations.

114 Energize the sacral chakra

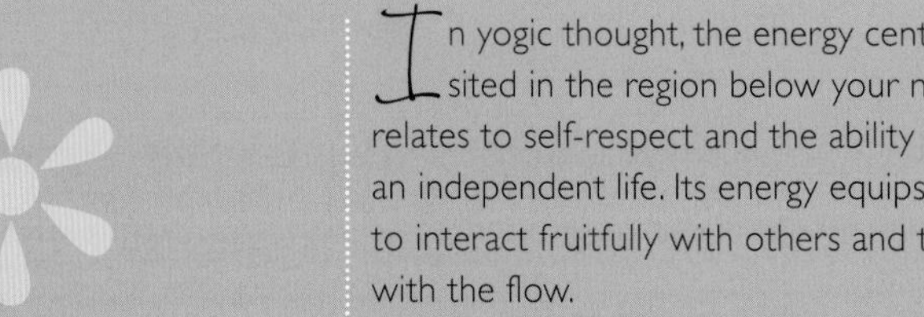

In yogic thought, the energy center sited in the region below your navel relates to self-respect and the ability to live an independent life. Its energy equips you to interact fruitfully with others and to go with the flow.

To develop your powers of give and take on your journey to greater wisdom, sit quietly and visualize your lower abdomen flooded with joyful orange light.

Plant some wise sage

115

Add a couple of sage plants to your herb garden or window box (the purple variety looks attractive and has more medicinal properties).

Sage earned its named for its stimulating tonic qualities and its ability to calm down the nervous system, promoting more considered decision-making. Use a few leaves in cooking; the flavor marries well with poultry dishes and savory squash or pumpkin recipes.

Instant wisdom

PEP UP YOUR EGGS
Chop a few fresh sage leaves and add them to your scrambled eggs.

116 Balloon-breathing

This exercise helps you to inhale and exhale more fully to maximize your intake of oxygen and output of carbon dioxide. This will help brain function.

Sit with your spine upright (supported by a wall if necessary), legs crossed comfortably and palms resting on your knees.

Close your eyes and watch your breath move in and out for a few breath cycles. Then imagine that you have a balloon in your abdomen. As you breathe in, slowly and steadily expand that balloon from the bottom up until your lungs are full. Pause for a moment, then very slowly let the balloon deflate from the top down until your lungs are completely empty. Repeat between three and five times.

Order is possible

117

If you struggle to keep your purse, workspace or home in order, take heart from the quotation below, which tells us that these skills can be cultivated. It's worth the effort; you'll feel organized and on top of things.

Why is it worth striving to do this? A recent study found that levels of cleanliness had a direct impact on students' ability to learn. Even spaces that were just casually untidy had a negative impact on learning.

Cleanliness and order are not matters of instinct; they are matters of education, and like most great things, you must cultivate a taste for them.

Benjamin Disraeli

118 Find your safe place

You have within you the reserves to comfort yourself when things aren't as good as you would like.

To call on this inborn wisdom, sit quietly in a warm place and close your eyes. Think back to a time when you felt well supported, perhaps floating in a calm sea or dozing on warm sand. Feel your muscles relax and the loss of tension as you breathe out.

Enjoy this moment. Once you have a 'body memory' of the experience, put words to it, such as 'warm' and 'soft'. Repeat them to yourself to link your body with the words. In future, repeating these words at times of difficulty will help to trigger the physical sensations of relaxation.

Cut it up

119

Owing money saps your inner wisdom. So if you constantly owe too much on credit cards, cut up one of them and dispose of the pieces in different places so you're not tempted to keep the number. Now work out how much you can afford to pay off each month and how many months it will take you to be free of this debt.

Put up shelves

120

Browse storage solutions in the shops and online today. You will need to acquire a set of shelves for your new collection of books if you are to turn your home into a haven of wisdom.

A room without books is like a body without a soul.

Marcus Tullius Cicero

121 Bedtime meditation

Wise thought

USE DAYLIGHT

Do the most brain-taxing tasks in daylight: the brain finds complex close-work challenging in the dark.

You probably have a far better understanding of what makes you tick by now, but try this evening meditation to draw these thoughts together.

As you lie in bed with your eyes closed, think about your body. Feel your limbs lying between the sheets and scan from your toes to the crown of your head. Is this you?

Now turn your thoughts to your emotions. Think back to any emotional outbursts today, or to times when you felt angry, sad or bored. Are any of these emotions really you? Now watch your mind for a while, telling itself stories. Is this really you? If none of these things are the essence of you, ask yourself what defines 'you'? Drift off to sleep on this thought.

Wise tale: 10 commandments

122

God appeared to Moses on Mount Sinai in a quake of thunder, lightning and trumpet sound. As the mountain smoked, God declared the rules of right living, commanding Moses to pass them on to his people. The commandments state, in essence, that there is no god but God, and that we should love God before all else, and love our neighbors as we love ourselves. As to the particulars, we should work hard for six days, but observe the seventh as a day of rest and worship. We should honor our parents, and never kill, but respect all living things. We should not commit adultery, steal or bear false witness against a neighbor, nor should we covet anyone or anything belonging to other people.

Wisdom: *people of all faiths can learn something about personal morality by contemplating these rules.*

checklist 4 How did you do?

Whether you tried out several ideas this month or just one, you might like to reflect on what you chose to try and why, and if it worked for you.

1. How many activities did you try this month?

- 1–3 activities ☐
- 4–10 activities ☐
- 11–20 activities ☐
- 21–30 activities ☐

2. How many did you repeat several times in the month?

- 1–3 activities ☐
- 4–10 activities ☐
- 11–20 activities ☐
- 21–30 activities ☐

3. Which activities had a positive effect on your sense of innate wisdom this month?

Use the page opposite to make notes about what worked for you and what didn't.

Notes, jottings and thoughts

123 Switch on autopilot

Wise thought

WRITE IT DOWN
Writing things down helps the brain to capture information and exercise its analytical powers.

On waking this morning, use your inbuilt wisdom to grant your unconscious mind permission to make a few decisions today. Tell your conscious mind to take a back seat.

Later, when faced with a question, try not to reason or judge consciously; instead, let your better self tell you what to do next.

Counting your breath

124

During your morning quiet time, sit comfortably, resting your hands on your knees, and watch your breath. This technique allows you to tap into your inner wisdom. Once your breathing feels steady and smooth, begin to count your in- and out-breaths.

Breathe in for a count of four and out for a count of four. When your mind wanders, keep returning to this steady count.

When you feel comfortable practicing this technique, hold your in-breath for another count of four before exhaling. Yogis believe that being able to control your breath is an essential step on the road to enlightenment.

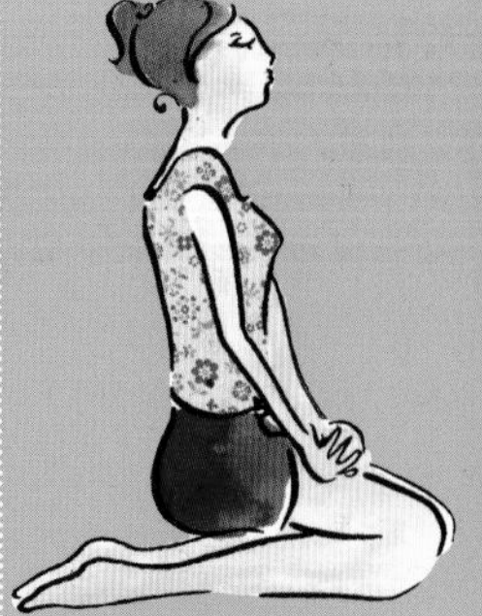

125 Eat some oats

Oats are fabulous food for the nervous system. They are a tonic for the body and uplifting for the mind, helping to counter the negative effects of stress and boost levels of energy and stamina.

Start your day with a good old-fashioned bowl of porridge sweetened with banana or apricots, or make your own muesli on a base of hearty jumbo oats.

Morning writing tune-in

126

Start your creative juices flowing before tackling tricky tasks today. Sit down with your journal and write a few sentences beneath one or two of the headings listed below. Don't scrutinize your words or even read them back if you don't want to. This exercise is not about achieving perfection, but about igniting your creative spark:

- My earliest memory
- The worst vacation ever
- What makes me laugh
- My grandparents' house.

Wise thought

SELF-DOUBT

Don't let fear stop you expressing yourself. The poet Sylvia Plath wrote that self-doubt is the worst enemy of creativity.

127 Block out two hours

To make intense brainwork or studying more efficient, carve out a two-hour block and fully concentrate on just one task. Don't check your emails, answer the phone or allow any other distractions to disturb you. Two hours is the optimum length of time for intense concentration, but don't worry if you haven't solved all the problems within that time slot.

Now switch to lighter tasks or take a walk or exercise class. During the down-time your unconscious mind will keep working on issues, delivering its insight in eureka moments. Try it; it really works!

Organize your desk

128

A desk strewn with papers and dirty coffee cups may be seen as the evidence of a spontaneous, creative mind, but it can also add minutes and unnecessary aggravation to your day when you are searching for hidden items.

Today, take everything off your desk. Wipe it clean, then replace only those items you will use today, such as your keyboard, phone, pen and notebook. Redistribute everything else to its proper place.

Instant wisdom

SPRITZ ENERGY
Add one or two drops of essential oil of lemongrass to the water in a pump spray and spritz your clean desk to energize your workplace. Lemongrass contains ingredients that clear the head and ease symptoms of stress.

129 Steer clear of gossip

Instant wisdom

EMOTIONAL MESSAGES

Ask what emotions, such as anger, are trying to tell you; there are clues in your past experiences of that emotion.

Try not to be tempted by the water-cooler crowd and the enticing web of workplace politics, scandal and rumor. It's simpler on the mind and conscience to approach everyone you encounter with an honest heart and being party to intrigue tends to make this less easy.

If you tell the truth you don't have to remember anything.

Mark Twain

Expansiveness meditation

130

Walk to a high place; the top of a tall building, a sea cliff or a hill. Sit down and just look out. Scan the picture in front of you for two or three minutes, getting a sense of the wider landscape and horizon. Then home in on figures or wildlife. Follow a particular figure going about their business. Can you understand their story?

Do this for about a minute. Think about your own life. Do you ignore the bigger picture, but get caught in the details? That's like following the figures and not seeing the big canvas. Finish by drawing your gaze back out to the horizon line and the landscape.

The voyage of discovery is not in seeking new landscapes but in having new eyes.

Marcel Proust

131 Let it all out

Fill your paper with the breathings of your heart.
William Wordsworth

If you enjoy writing, but lack inspiration, call on the Three Muses. These are the daughters of the Greek god Zeus, to whom writers and artists have turned for centuries to bring their work to life.

First invoke Melete, or meditation, by allowing any subject, object, snatch of conversation or thought to spark a response in you. You might hear two people saying something interesting on the train, witness an altercation between a dog and a cat or remember a scene from your childhood. Reflect on this; become completely involved.

Then turn to Mneme, or remembrance. What feelings do these events stimulate in you? Try to empathize with your subjects. When you have brought them to life, ask the third muse, Aoede, or song, for help in getting it down on paper in a distinct voice.

Clothes make the person

132

Choose an outfit today that projects an image to the world of how you would like to feel. You'll be adding to your 'wisdom bank' by being the person you really want to be.

Are you an in-control executive, a creative thinker, an earth-mother or a geek today? Who have you always wanted to be? Shout it to the world and notice whether co-workers and friends treat you differently.

Instant wisdom

DRESS WISE

What's the timeless uniform of the wise? Channel the left-bank Paris of Jean-Paul Sartre and Simone de Beauvoir by wearing fitted black sweaters, pedal-pushers and matelot stripes with ballet slippers.

133 The joy of idling

Try to engineer your schedule so you get the chance to do nothing this afternoon. It will really pay dividends on the wisdom front. Take a long bath, listen to music, get a massage or go to bed with your lover.

Stepping off the regular merry-go-round makes your body and mind more stress-resistant and boosts your ability to perform with concentration and efficiency. Repeat this every two weeks.

Take rest; a field that has rested gives a bountiful crop.

Ovid

Tell the truth

134

Today, be a little more aware than usual of what you say. Watch whether you tell white lies, augment the truth or fail to speak out when you know you should. Being a wiser person is about being more honest in your relationships and dealings with other people.

A half truth is a whole lie.

Yiddish proverb

Time for nuts

135

Walnuts resemble tiny brains; have you noticed? This is appropriate because they have been shown to help in the fight against cognitive decline and to keep mood swings at bay. Have a handful as a mid-morning snack.

136 Relax on your front

Tension is who you think you should be. Relaxation is who you are.

Chinese proverb

We tend to relax lying on our backs or lounging on our sides. But lying on the front of the body brings a new awareness and sense of grounding to relaxation, which adds to our store of knowledge about the body.

To try this, lie on your front with your legs hip-width apart and big toes touching (let your heels drop outward). Fold your arms in front of your head, stacking palms. Rest your forehead or one cheek on your top hand. Close your eyes and relax. Feel your belly expand, pressing into the floor, as you breathe in. As you breathe out, let the front of your body relax into the safe support of the floor. Rest here for up to five minutes, changing cheeks, if necessary. Push back to rest your buttocks on your heels, keeping your head down, before sitting up slowly.

Recruit an exercise buddy

137

All of us find it difficult to keep to our good exercise intentions; a must since aerobic exercise has been shown to build brain power.

So recruit a fitness friend today and exchange your fitness plans. How can you encourage each other to get to class or wake early enough to walk to work? Could you spend 30 minutes power-walking together at lunchtime or share the cost of a personal trainer or yoga teacher? A workout buddy makes you feel obliged when it would be easy to stay sedentary.

138 Train outdoors

Instant wisdom

JUST PLAY!

In sports, practice the techniques so thoroughly that when you hit the court or pitch you can forget the rudiments, relax and just play. This is a wise move!

Studies suggest that people who exercise outside are more likely to stick to an exercise regime, so today plan an outdoor activity session. Theories suggest this is because spending time in green spaces makes us feel calmer, better balanced and more energized (it's even been called 'vitamin G' for its positive effect on healing and longevity).

Live in the sunshine, swim the sea, drink the wild air

Ralph Waldo Emerson

Try a Forward Bend

139

This exercise rests the heart and lungs, which can help to raise energy levels and increase clear thinking during a long day. Stand arm's length from a wall, facing it. Place your feet hip-width apart, parallel to each other. Lift up from your ankles as in Mountain Pose (see page 26) and extend your arms overhead. Hold for a few breaths in and out. Exhaling, pivot forward from your hips and rest your palms on the wall so that your body makes an inverted L-shape. Rest here for up to a minute, feeling the stretch in the backs of your legs and your spine.

After a few weeks' practice, let your upper body drop toward the floor, folding your arms and relaxing the back of your neck (avoid this if you have high blood pressure). Come back to standing gradually.

140 Buy a fair-trade lunch

Flex your ethical acumen this lunchtime by changing your regular choice of food to an item bearing a fair-trade sticker. This can be as seemingly inconsequential as an ordinary banana, a cup of coffee or a slab of chocolate.

Read the label or look up the website and think about how your consumer choices can affect the working conditions and family lives of people on the other side of the world. This is a wise act.

The bigger picture

141

Plan a trip to an awe-inspiring landscape. Human beings seem to have an innate need to spend time in places where our own lives are dwarfed by awesome natural phenomena.

Being faced with a cliff to climb or a fast-flowing stream to cross throws our troubles into perspective, halting, for a moment, our preoccupation with ourselves.

Research has found that the closer we feel to nature, the higher the increase in self-esteem and inner wisdom. Wilderness experiences have been shown to fulfil our need to be challenged and excited while teaching vital life skills such as good judgment, tenacity and compassion.

Instant wisdom

OUTDOOR CHALLENGE

Enrol on a wilderness challenge, such as an outward-bound or bushcraft course.

142 Leave your wallet at home

Today leave home without any money or credit cards. Can you survive a day without spending?

You'll probably need a packed lunch and a flask of coffee, but what can you find to do that's free? Go for a walk? Visit a gallery? Once you start using your initiative, endless options will present themselves to you.

Wise books

143

Today, pick up a book and read for the sheer pleasure of it. Evidence suggests that reading books as a leisure activity increases general knowledge, widens vocabulary and increases the ability to write. It also combats loneliness, enhances social skills and offers insight into human nature and decision-making.

Whenever you can, read in front of a child. Modeling wise behavior is the best way to set children up for a lifetime of enjoyable learning, personal growth and entertainment.

Love of learning is akin to wisdom.

Confucius

144 Start a nature table

Ayurveda, the Indian system of healthcare, and naturopathy, the complementary health system, both teach that when we live according to the cycle of the seasons, our bodies become better balanced and we are more able to cope with stress.

To start becoming more nature-wise, today bring home one seasonal object you find, to remind you of the turning of the year. It might be a leaf, a pine cone, a piece of bark or a feather. Avoid picking wild flowers. Place the object on a table with sketches of your findings or wildlife books open at the appropriate page.

Cook seasonally

145

Buy or borrow a seasonal cookbook and plan a meal made mostly of seasonal ingredients. You don't have to be a vegetarian to do this: meat, fish, shellfish and game all have seasons, too.

Challenge yourself to cook seasonally once a week. The most enjoyable way to gain this knowledge is to make a weekly visit to a farmer's market or get a regular organic box delivered to your door. You can watch the local produce change as the year rolls on. Watch the prices fall, too. Produce that is in season will be plentiful as well as fresh, and therefore cheaper.

Instant wisdom

ONLINE HELP
Bookmark a seasonal cooking site and sign up for weekly email alerts about which ingredients are at their freshest.

146 Shrink your thoughts

Before bed, sit quietly with your eyes closed watching your thoughts pass, as if they were pictures projected on a screen. Try to watch them with disinterest. After a while, shrink the screen and turn the pictures to black and white. Turn down the sound, too. Let your mind enjoy the relaxing darkness.

147 Bedtime thanksgiving

Make the last thing you do today a thanksgiving for the day; for the good things such as food, company and relationships. Give thanks, too, for the chance to learn and grow when faced with bad news. Go to sleep with these thoughts circulating in your brain. Sleep well!

Bake bread

148

We deprive ourselves of one of life's great pleasures when we eat industrially processed, plastic-wrapped bread. And the additives, flour-improvers and processing aids in these loaves don't help our quest to live more honestly.

Become more discerning this morning by stocking up on the two ingredients you need to bake a simple loaf at home: bread flour and yeast (you'll have the other two already: water and salt). Then look up a recipe and bake a delicious home-made loaf this afternoon.

149 Seeing in detail

The Romantic poets and writers believed that engaging with landscape helped them to form a discerning intelligence. Today, look at a small detail in the landscape, perhaps at a single petal or the movement of water. Then describe it using words or watercolors. Try this as often as you can. It's easier with practice.

Nursed amidst the grandeur of mountain scenery, he has stooped to have a nearer view of the daisy under his feet or plucked a branch of white-thorn from the spray. And in describing it, his mind seems imbued with the majesty and solemnity of the objects around him.

William Hazlitt on William Wordsworth

Join a book club

150

Browse noticeboards at work, your local library or arts center for a book club. You'll find that belonging to one enhances your wisdom in several ways. Book clubs are friendly little groups and a safe place to begin expressing your opinions in public and to practice your listening skills.

Members meet informally to discuss a book, usually once a month, and everyone gets to make a choice of book. Call the contact number today and commit yourself to the next meeting, to start expanding your horizons and extending your range of reading matter.

151 Waking naturally

Instant wisdom

EARLY BIRD
To feel extra productive and get you off to a good start, tackle the worst job of the day early in the morning.

To hone your awareness of your innate capabilities and your inbuilt body wisdom, tonight don't set your alarm and trust yourself to wake naturally tomorrow. It's best to do this on a day when you don't have any responsibilities to attend to first thing!

Get up shortly after you first wake rather than dozing off again, which may help you tune in to your internal body clock. If you oversleep, think about shifting your bedtime earlier or examine whether parts of your life are overtiring you.

Wise tale: the wandering poet

152

Named for the banana plant outside his hut, the 17th-century Japanese poet Basho was made homeless after the hut burnt down. He had no family and so, for the sake of his spiritual life and his writing, decided to become a wanderer. He set off on foot to visit far-away provinces and mountain ranges, compiling a travel journal which reveals his development both as a poet and a spiritual being. As he immersed himself in nature, allowing its sublime grandeur and constant, yet ever-changing, qualities to blot out his ego, the wayfarer became more serene, able to experience life in the moment and express something of its unknowable form.

Wisdom: *immersion in nature brings a lightness of spirit and creative inspiration that allows us to engage with the world with greater understanding and compassion.*

checklist 5 How did you do?

Whether you tried out several ideas this month or just one, you might like to reflect on what you chose to try and why, and if it worked for you.

1. How many activities did you try this month?

- 1–3 activities ☐
- 4–10 activities ☐
- 11–20 activities ☐
- 21–30 activities ☐

2. How many did you repeat several times in the month?

- 1–3 activities ☐
- 4–10 activities ☐
- 11–20 activities ☐
- 21–30 activities ☐

3. Which activities had a positive effect on your sense of innate wisdom this month?

Use the page opposite to make notes about what worked for you and what didn't.

Notes, jottings and thoughts

153 Kneeling for meditation

A kneeling position is thought, in some traditions, to make meditation easier, since it positions the spine and head in such a way that the meditator remains alert and engaged.

Fold a blanket and kneel with your knees and feet touching and well cushioned by the blanket. Now sink your buttocks onto your heels, allowing your body weight to drop down through your hips and feet. If this is uncomfortable, place one cushion beneath your feet and another beneath your buttocks. Sit upright and rest your hands on your thighs. Close your eyes and begin your meditation. With daily practice, notice how sitting becomes more effortless.

Bus-stop meditation

154

If waiting depletes your sense of wisdom, try this meditation to arrive at work cool and collected. First disengage from your emotions by watching them as if you were a bystander. Notice how your mind and heartbeat are racing, your fists and jaw are clenched or your neck and shoulders stiff. Who is this tense person? Not the wise you inside. Now let that real you out. Breathe in; as you breathe out imagine your mind dropping into the back of your head. Breathe in again and, as you exhale, send waves of calmness to envelop your heart. Then inhale and, as you exhale, drop and broaden your shoulders. Repeat, this time releasing clenched fingers and toes. Remain disengaged, eyeing your body with curiosity until the train or bus arrives.

155 Be streetwise

Wise thought

THINK AHEAD
Before attending an interview or a new job, make enquiries about the dress code.

If you lack confidence when out and about and it stops you from visiting new places or meeting new people, try the following tips to make you feel and look more street-savvy.

First lift your chin when you walk, look ahead and relax your shoulders away from your ears. Increase the speed with which you walk, without hurrying, and keep your gait smooth, allowing your arms to swing with fluidity.

Look at the world around you, being aware of what's going on and the others around you. Make eye contact with those you meet. You'll feel more in command of your body, more purposeful and therefore wiser.

Interpreting dreams

156

Set aside a spare 30 minutes and sit somewhere cosy to read your dream journal (see Day 65, page 75). Keep a pen and paper handy. Read through your dreams and jot down random thoughts. Can you spot any patterns? Which areas of life do your dreams seem to be addressing? Do any obvious interpretations spring to mind? What is the imagery telling you?

Pay attention to the emotions evoked. Dreams can't be adequately interpreted by dream-symbol books; they need your subjective input to 'unlock' their private messages and turn them into useful pointers. For example, dreaming about being lost in a maze might indicate that you are seeking answers, but only you hold the missing key that can tell you what the questions are.

157 Try Downward Dog

Inverting the body is thought to increase intellectual clarity and emotional stability by calming the head and energizing the heart, so why not try the classic Downward Dog yoga pose?

Start on your hands and knees. Breathing out, press into your palms and straighten your legs, pressing your buttocks backward and toward the ceiling. Push your armpits toward your knees and relax your neck. Hold for 30–60 seconds, drop back to hands and knees, then sit back on your heels.

Keep on keeping on

158

If you feel like giving up on a task or person today, sit quietly for a minute. Close your eyes and watch your breath until it is moving calmly in and out of your lungs. Now tune into the reasons why you decided to embark on this quest. Think about your 'big-picture' goals, then the practical ways you decided to change the small things in your life. How does today's struggle connect to these aims? What small step could you take to get back on track? Open your eyes, stand up, breathe out all the way, take a refreshing in-breath and tackle it now.

To get through the hardest journey we need take only one step at a time, but we must keep on stepping.

Chinese proverb

159 Memory game

Wise thought

TRAIN YOUR MEMORY

To promote a good memory, organize thoughts into categories of knowledge: the mind likes ideas to be filed away neatly.

Increase your memory skills by 'elaborative encoding': putting a narrative to random words you have to remember. This could be co-workers' names or a shopping list. It works by fixing the information in your long-term memory.

Try it now: think of 12 random words and write them down. Try to memorize the list, turn it over and see if you can recall the words. How many stick in your mind? Now make another list of 12 random words. Invent a story in which all the words feature, such as 'On a blue moon, my sister went to the shop to buy a tree. But when she got there, the door was locked and she had an ice-cream instead, which dripped on her new shoes'. Turn the paper over and try to remember all 12 words. See how much easier your recall is.

Shop with farmers

160

Take a walk to the farmers' market at lunchtime and buy yourself a locally grown lunch and supper. As you browse the stalls ask questions about how best to combine and cook the ingredients, and ask about how stock is raised and how crops are grown.

This is a wise way to go, not only for your health and the health of the land (buying local is green because it cuts down on transportation and refrigeration); it's also a wiser choice for your region, since it keeps money within the local economy.

161 *Wise up*

Today, assess your judgment of a potentially tricky situation against other people's assessments of it.

On the left-hand side of a sheet of paper list your reasons for feeling wronged or aggrieved. Look at recent issues and more long-standing grievances.

On the right-hand side list the other person's point of view. Which interpretation is correct? Can you list any common ground in the center of the paper?

Patience, patience

162

Memorize the quotation below today. When you find yourself getting angry or frustrated, repeat it as a wise mantra. Try to coordinate the words with your breathing. Say the word 'patience' to yourself as you breathe in and complete the sentence as you breathe out. Even if the words seem to have little meaning for you, lengthening your exhalations and deepening your inhalations will make you feel calmer and more in control of a situation.

Patience is the companion of wisdom.

St Augustine

Instant wisdom

GINKGO

This ancient plant has long been used in China as a memory and concentration enhancer.

163 Value others

Instant wisdom

WISE PERSON
Do an online image search for your wise person of choice and use the picture as your screensaver.

Meditate on the value and equality of all living beings, whatever their status, by thinking about the haiku below, written by the Japanese poet Issa. In this piece of writing, the poet and the insect are given equal status. The man is no more important than the fly. Compare this viewpoint to your regular way of thinking about the creepy-crawlies in your own home and about the way you view animals in the food chain. Does this encourage you to respect our fellow creatures more and perhaps buy free-range eggs or pork from pigs raised where they can forage and move around freely?

Just one man
and one fly
in this huge drawing room.

Issa

Drink more water

164

Dehydration of the body can lead to an approximate ten per cent deterioration in memory, concentration and attention span. Thirst can also make you feel irritated and tired. Aim to drink between six and eight medium-sized glasses of water today and every day: more if it's hot or you are physically active.

Pin up a postcard

165

Search for a photograph or portrait of a wise person and pin it above your desk, in your kitchen or near your bed. Let it inspire you to find out more about that person's life and good works. Good choices might include The Buddha, Mother Teresa, Mahatma Gandhi or Joan of Arc.

166 Extend a hand

All the world's great religions teach that wisdom is more than being well-intentioned in our own lives; it's about reaching out to others. This is one of the most difficult must-dos on any journey to a better life, but try to get started today. Help someone who needs a hand or try to make amends for a past injustice.

Love thy neighbor as thyself.
Do not do to others what thou wouldst not wish be done to thyself.
Forgive injuries. Forgive thy enemy, be reconciled to him, give him assistance, invoke God in his behalf.

Confucius

Leave work on time

167

Part of wise time management is making space for activities and people you love after your workday is done. To make sure you leave the workplace at a reasonable time, make commitments that it's difficult to cancel last minute: book a dental appointment, theater ticket or sign up for a regular exercise or language class.

168 Think while you walk

Take a 30-minute walk every day. It's important for your health and wellbeing and it gives you time alone to reflect. If you need motivation to fuel your daily walk, read how it influenced one of the leading thinkers of the 20th century:

Above all, do not lose your desire to walk. Every day I walk myself into a state of well-being and walk away from every illness. I have walked myself into my best thoughts, and I know of no thought so burdensome that one cannot walk away from it.

Soren Kierkegaard

Meditate after work

169

When you come in from work, after you have taken off your coat, bag and shoes, wipe the stress from your day with ten or 20 minutes' meditation before greeting your loved ones.

Set the timer on your phone and sit quietly. Either count your breath or use one of your favorite meditations or visualization exercises from previous days. Then enjoy your evening. Notice how switching-off time transforms your after-work conversation from negative griping to more positive engagement.

Wise thought

KEEP ENGAGED
Divide your work day into distinct chunks and mix up tasks and subjects to keep your brain active and engaged.

170 Boycott fast fashion

Make your choice of clothing a little wiser by avoiding budget fashion shops this month. Can you save the money you would usually spend on clothing or accessories and purchase one beautiful, ethically produced item that you love enough to wear forever?

Ethically produced means created by a craftsperson or made in places that have strict legislation governing fair pay and conditions for garment workers.

Wise thought

BUY DESIGNER

Many high-end fashion labels source and create garments ethically, so don't feel guilty about buying designer and supporting independent boutiques.

Sketchbook journal

171

Pop out this lunchtime with a sketchbook and pencil. Sit in a quiet place for ten minutes and draw a plant; it doesn't have to be beautiful. Many weeds have a fascinating structure and habits of growth. Don't worry if you can't draw; this is a way of stopping, really looking and opening yourself up to the natural world. As you become engrossed in replicating the intricate details of nature, do you feel greater insight into the world around you?

We cannot remember too often that when we observe nature, and especially the ordering of nature, it is always ourselves alone we are observing.

Georg Christoph Lichtenberg

172 Savvy shopper

Are you 'brandwashed?' Do you automatically opt for an item from the supermarket shelf just because you recognize the logo? Do you want that new bag for its shape, its color or for the name it sports? Try to be more experimental and free-thinking today. Buy a non-branded or own-label product and be proud of it. The wise dare to stand proudly alone!

He goes by the brand, yet imagines he goes by the flavor.

Mark Twain

Managing your time

173

How long do the tasks you do most days usually take? Now look at the week ahead. What do you have to do and how long do you predict it will take?

If your tasks take much longer than the allotted time, how could you resolve the mismatch? Are there tasks you could jettison or delegate? Could you speak to your partner or manager about solutions? If your tasks are home-based, could you ask others to help you with them and share some of the responsibility?

If you don't have enough time for family and friends, get up 30 minutes earlier tomorrow to breakfast together or meet at an early-bird meditation class.

174 Time for everything

We are all subject to time; the wise don't rail against time passing, but grasp its opportunities as they run by, choosing which experiences to keep and build on and which to let go of. Look up the following wise words in *The Bible*, then copy them out and pin them up:

To everything there is a season,
and a time to every purpose under
heaven: A time to be born, and a
time to die; a time to plant, and
a time to pluck up that which is
planted; A time to kill, and a
time to heal; a time to break
down, and a time to build up;
A time to weep, and a time to
laugh; a time to mourn,
and a time to dance...

Ecclesiastes 3:1–8

Play with children

175

There's no better way of switching off from work than playing with children. They tend to live in the moment, enjoying what's happening here and now rather than running over past wrongs or anticipating future problems, like adults tend to. Tell children that for 30 minutes you will play whatever they like, and then do whatever they say. (No answering phones, playing with Blackberries or trying to read a magazine!)

Wise thought

BE WITH CHILDREN

If you don't have children or godchildren of your own, why not volunteer for a children's charity, try some babysitting or help out in a classroom, listening to children read?

176

Eat more eggs

Eggs contain choline, known as the 'memory vitamin' for its ability to act on the brain centers that are connected with learning and memory. Choline is especially important for the developing brain, so if you have children, why not start the day with French toast?

177

Walk even more

Thoughts come clearly while one walks.

Thomas Mann

Today, take a longer walk than usual. Walking is one of the best ways of boosting your mental acuity and more contemplative thinking. Invest in a detailed walkers' map and plan a route that goes past monuments or nature reserves: they can add to your personal store of wisdom.

Practice saying 'no'

178

This part of the journey toward greater wisdom focuses on our relationship with others. This doesn't just mean turning into a better listener or becoming more compassionate, it means knowing when to say 'no' to excessive demands on your time or emotions.

Today, when you want to say 'no', take a step back to assess the situation and personalities from a more neutral standpoint. Why is it difficult to say 'no'? Is it because you want to please? Why might this be? Is it because you don't respect your own need for rest and recuperation? Think about how much better it is to say 'no' now than letting someone down later or turning in poor work because you were too busy to do the task justice.

179 Try Iyengar yoga

This form of yoga shows you how to use your innate intelligence as you move. When you hold a pose, you are asked to take your 'intelligence' into every part of your body evenly, from extremities such as your fingertips and toes to your internal organs.

With practice, you learn to observe every part of the body simultaneously and the subtle changes taking place there, and understand how to use your intelligence to adjust and readjust until nothing internal or external disturbs you. This is meditation.

Bedtime reading

180

The following novels are not just compelling page-turners, but each contains profound messages and wisdom. Enjoy them before bed:

- *A Christmas Carol*, Charles Dickens: miser sees the error of his ways.
- *The Shack*, William P Young: a man spends a weekend with God.
- *Autobiography of a Yogi*, Parahamsa Yogananda: enlightening meetings with gurus.
- *Mutant Message Downunder*, Marlo Morgan: businesswoman abandons her shoulder pads to wander the Australian outback.
- *Beloved*, Toni Morrison: memory, suffering and a haunting ghost story.

181 Home filing system

Instant wisdom

GO FOR COMPLETION
Finish one job before moving on to another.

This evening take out all the papers you tend to push to one side, such as insurance policies, health certificates, utility bills, warranties, instruction booklets and wills.

Organize like with like, then sort by date. How many of these pieces of paper are defunct or relate to appliances or policies you gave up long ago? Burn or shred these. Place all current documents in each pile into a separate folder with a clear label. Now find a place for them, not hidden in a garage or loft, but easily accessible. How much wiser do you feel now?

Wise tale: a flower sermon

182

The Buddha was preparing to give a sermon to his disciples on Mount Grdhakuta. There was great anticipation about which stories and how many wise thoughts he would relate. The time came when The Buddha was to begin. But instead of talking, he simply held up a flower, which had transfixed him as he was preparing his sermon. He held the flower before his listeners, turning it in his fingers. All the disciples were puzzled except one, who eventually smiled. He understood the truth that lies both beyond words and the act of teaching. His name was Mahakashyapa. Then The Buddha spoke, saying, 'I have said all I can to you disciples; what cannot be said I entrust to Mahakashyapa.'

Wisdom: *what can direct experience rather than study and fine words teach us about the nature of truth?*

checklist 6 How did you do?

Whether you tried out several ideas this month or just one, you might like to reflect on what you chose to try and why, and if it worked for you.

1. How many activities did you try this month?

- 1–3 activities ☐
- 4–10 activities ☐
- 11–20 activities ☐
- 21–30 activities ☐

2. How many did you repeat several times in the month?

- 1–3 activities ☐
- 4–10 activities ☐
- 11–20 activities ☐
- 21–30 activities ☐

3. Which activities had a positive effect on your sense of innate wisdom this month?

Use the page opposite to make notes about what worked for you and what didn't.

Notes, jottings and thoughts

183 A room of one's own

Instant wisdom

FOCUS FOR THOUGHTS

Make a display of photographs, paintings or spiritual symbols that remind you of your journey, and light a candle to represent light in the darkness.

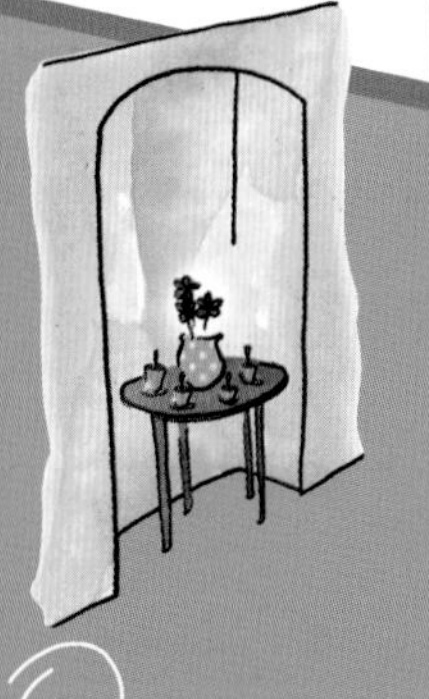

Prove to the world that you are taking your interior life seriously by dedicating a small part of your home to yoga or meditation practice.

The area doesn't need to be very large, just enough space to stretch out your arms overhead and to the sides, but it does need to be a place where you can carry out your practice undisturbed and in warmth. Try to keep your yoga mat, cushions and blankets in this place permanently.

Try the Chair Twist

184

Rotating the spinal column has a rejuvenating effect on the nerves and abdominal organs and eases neck and shoulder pain.

Sit side-on to a chair with no arms, with your side against one side of the chair-back and feet flat on the floor, shoulder-width apart. Breathe in and extend your spine. Breathing out, start to turn toward the chair-back from your lower abdomen.

When you feel a good twist here, continue turning your shoulders and take your hands to the chair back. Look over your shoulder. Hold for 30–60 seconds. Inhaling, turn back to center. Change position and repeat to the other side.

185 Warming up

Use this dance warm-up in the morning to unite your body gently with your awareness. Turn on some music that has a slow but steady beat.

First warm up your joints by circling your ankles, knees, hips and shoulders and by turning your head. Then march on the spot, exaggerating your arm and leg movements to warm your muscles. Now spot five points in space and make up a flowing sequence of movements, during which you touch those spots over and over with different parts of your body. Let your movements flow with the slow, steady beat. This warms up the nerve fibers, linking muscles and brain commands, making every movement that follows more accurate.

So-hum meditation

186

As you sit quietly this morning watching your breath moving in and out, start to notice the sound of the air moving in your throat. Observe how it seems to say *so* on the in-breath and *hum* on the out-breath. Become absorbed in these sounds for a few minutes.

In the divinely revealed language Sanskrit, *so* can be translated as 'I am' and *hum* translated as 'that'. To utter it is to connect yourself with everything that is outside yourself; every other creature that breathes and the life force that animates them.

187 Try expert instruction

Were you terrified of sport at school? Do you still shun team games on the beach or in the park? Take heart. This gives you a head start in learning sports skills over those who are naturally athletic. Because you acknowledge your limitations, such as stiffness or lack of co-ordination, you are more likely to listen to instruction, attend to the details and keep your mind engaged with the new actions, working methodically and consciously until you 'get it'. So today, book a try-out lesson in a new activity that requires expert tutelage, such as ice skating, bowling or golf.

Ask for an opinion

188

Instead of going about your business as usual, this morning ask someone's opinion about a choice you are making. It could be as you decide what to buy in the supermarket, worry over a work problem, or ponder where to take a toddler to play.

Act on that person's advice. Being wise means putting your ego aside, taking on board the opinions of others and then acting on them.

Wise thought

LISTEN UP!

To become a better listener keep your mouth closed when someone is talking; if necessary, rest one finger on your lips.

189 Speaking too much

The wise ones fashioned speech with their thought, sifting it as grain is sifted through a sieve.

The Buddha

If you are a chatterbox by nature and would like to ponder your thoughts more before letting them spill out (which is what wise people do), try the following energy-concentration technique.

When you feel fit to burst with gossip, sit up straight and lift your breastbone. Very gently lower your chin toward your chest without letting your chest drop. Don't worry if your chin doesn't reach your chest; don't force it, just enjoy the stretch at the back of your neck. Yogis believe that this helps to keep emotional responses in your chest rather than rising to your head.

Your throat chakra

190

In yogic thought, the energy center at the front of the neck relates to how honestly we express ourselves.

To develop your ability to listen to what you truly believe, make wise choices based on this and express those decisions to others, sit quietly and visualize this area of your body bathed in sky-blue light.

191

Sky dreaming

Buddhists believe that the way to enlightenment is meditation. Try out this easy form, which is a bit like daydreaming:

Lie on your back on a patch of grass for five minutes. Look up and watch the clouds passing. When thoughts occur, imagine them as clouds passing over and let them go without feeling guilty, trapped or intrigued. As each new cloud comes, let it go. After five minutes feel the solid earth supporting you and imagine your heavy bones sinking into it and your muscles releasing their tension. Roll to one side to rest and then to the other before sitting up.

Meander time

192

Wisdom is so much more than remembering dates and complex facts. Today, tune in to your instinctive intelligence; the type of knowledge that provides the answers to questions in dreams. This weekend, go for an aimless walk. Don't have a destination or a set route in mind. Just let your instinct decide which direction to take at a crossroads. Think of it as physical daydreaming. Walk like this for ten minutes, then make your way back, mulling over any thoughts that arose.

Time is but the stream I go a-fishing in.

Henry David Thoreau

193 Think before you speak

Today, try to engage your innate kindness before speaking. Don't let unkind words pass your lips.

It's ancient advice, but it always helps to take a deep breath in and then out and count to ten before uttering a word in anger. If you need to, leave the room or terminate a phone call before your instinct to gossip or curse cuts in.

Speech is the mirror of the soul; as a man speaks, so is he.

Publilius Syrus

Lose your watch

194

To see how aligned you are with the outside world, leave home without wearing your watch today. See if you can intuit lunchtime and coffee breaks. Practice gauging an hour and tune in to other sources of timekeeping, such as the height of the sun, the placement of shadows and the chiming of church clocks.

Time discovers truth.

Seneca

Surprise your palate

195

Eat something unusual for breakfast. Try a slice of papaya with lime juice, a new herbal tea, vegetable soup or a salad. The more diverse foods you build into your day, the more healthy your diet will be. And the more new activities you try, the more active your brain will stay as you age.

196 Think about relationships

Instant wisdom

TALK TALK
Have a conversation tonight rather than dozing in front of the TV.

You already know what it would take to improve your relationship with significant others in your life. Get that wisdom down on paper.

List each of your significant relationships: parents, siblings, boss, partner and friends. Next to each one write down how you could improve that connection. Try to make them concrete actions, such as, 'Call them once a week' or 'Give back the shoes I borrowed'. Try to make a start on one action today.

Be more money-wise

197

Now is the time to set your accounts in order by beginning to pay off a debt. Set up a debit direct from your bank account each month to a debtor or credit-card company.

It can be useful to take advice on how much to pay back each month to stop interest from spiraling out of control, and on which debts to prioritize.

Paying of debts is, next to the grace of God, the best means in the world to deliver you from a thousand temptations to sin and vanity.

Patrick Delany

198 Deal with difficult people

When dealing with difficult personalities, the wise person trusts that they are rational beings with the best of motives and assumes things will turn out for the good. This can be problematic, of course, since it involves switching off regular and quite reasonable responses. But approaching the world with anger and negativity only breeds more of the same. Try being positive and helpful today and watch how this habit, too, spreads to those around you.

When we treat man as he is, we make him worse than he is; when we treat him as if he already were what he potentially could be, we make him what he should be.

Goethe

Clear some clutter

199

If you're happy to live in a cluttered home, great! But if accumulated stuff makes life more difficult than it should be, befuddles your brain or darkens emotions with negativity, it's time to cut clutter.

Keep your expectations realistic. Today just tackle one corner of a room and then plan to deal with another area next week. Why not organize a garage sale or take your things to your local thrift store?

200 Have a hug!

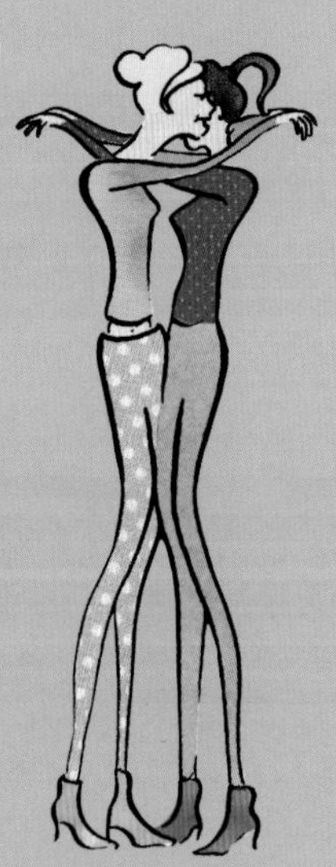

It's too easy to race around getting everything done and forget to nurture those we love. So make time today to give your loved ones a special hug.

Body and mind respond well to such positive touch. In studies, it was found that even a short hug made people feel happier and more relaxed. Hugging also seems to benefit blood pressure, to help us deal with stress and to keep the brain alert and doing well in skills such as math computation. Hugging also boosts IQ and language skills in children. What better way of making all of us mentally and emotionally wiser?

Just one tipple

201

Drinking more than the amount of alcohol that is recommended for your age and gender can make your brain physically smaller!

Try to stick to the recommended limits; one study defined 'heavy drinking' as more than 14 alcoholic drinks a week. For optimum health benefits, the World Health Organization recommends no more than one glass a day, but it's good to have a few alcohol-free days each week, too.

202 Enjoy singing

Give your throat chakra exercise by expressing yourself with your voice. Yogis believe that this leads to more honest and positive connections with those around you; wise people actively create more close-knit communities.

Try this out as you potter around your home this evening. Breathe in, then breathe out and relax your shoulders and abdomen. Take another deep breath in, open your mouth wide and let the breath out as the sound 'AAAA'. Feel the sound powered by your abdomen and enjoy the vibrations tickling your throat. Repeat as often as you like, stopping if you feel light-headed.

Cook for a friend

203

People who share meals with family and friends tend to eat more healthily and have a good social support system; both are key to keeping us happy and mentally bright.

Invite someone to dine tonight and cook for them from scratch. Keep the TV switched off so that you can nurture good conversation.

Wise thought

COOKING SWAP

If you cook tonight, arrange a regular swap so someone else cooks for you next week.

204 Make mayonnaise

Wise thought

ETHICAL EGGS

For ethical peace of mind, choose free-range eggs, preferably from a chicken owner you know and trust.

You can't double-task or only half pay attention when making mayonnaise. Your body and mind have to stay fully engaged from start to finish as you drip in the oil and keep stirring in the same direction. This makes it a form of mindfulness, or meditation-in-motion.

Ingredients: 1 teaspoon sea salt; yolk of 1 large free-range, very fresh egg; approximately 200 ml (6 fl oz) extra-virgin olive oil; juice of half a lemon.

Pound the salt in a pestle and mortar, then stir in the egg yolk. Drop by drop, add the oil, stirring constantly in one direction with a wooden spoon until the mixture forms peaks and no more oil can be absorbed. Stir in the lemon juice, to taste, before serving. Note: avoid eating mayonnaise if you are pregnant or have impaired immunity.

Go dancing

205

After work try a dance class that teaches a formal dance involving memorizing patterns of movements, forward and backward actions, step sequences and reacting to a partner.

All these actions serve to stimulate the brain, while socializing makes you a more wise and compassionate person. Dances that involve frequent twisting movements, such as the tango or salsa, provide even better mental stimulation.

206 Listen to the classics

As an evening wind-down put on a piece of classical music and sit and listen to it. Don't do chores or chat at the same time, just listen. If this is new to you, Mozart's 'Prussian Quartets' for cello are a good place to start. This composer's music is famed for being able to raise IQ and boost concentration span and memory.

207 Reverse gear

If your brain feels fuggy this afternoon, stand up and walk backward across the room. Separate brain systems control the patterns of walking forward and backward, and switching from one to the other helps to make you feel both refreshed and rejuvenated.

Start a blog

208

Do you have an unfulfilled desire to gain experience in a new field? Perhaps by climbing a mountain, traveling to far-flung parts or following in the footsteps of a historical figure?

To build up the courage to undertake such a great feat, blog about it. Explain the nature of your desire in the first entry, why you feel compelled to complete this challenge, then list the likely pitfalls. Send links to key supportive friends and ask them to pass on the site address to others. Having the world urging you on will heighten your motivation to seek out this wisdom.

209 Unfocused gaze

Before bed tonight, practice unfocusing your gaze. Counter-intuitively, this focuses concentration. In yoga, it is said that the mind follows where the eyes focus, and so we are urged to direct our gaze not at outside objects (which draws thoughts and energy to those objects) but within the self.

Sit quietly, with your chest lifted and the back of your neck long. Keep your eyes open and look ahead, but widen and soften your gaze so that no one object is in focus. Now imagine gazing at your third eye in the center of your forehead. Don't actually do this with your eyes, just visualize it. Finally, direct your gaze toward the back of your head. Try your best to hold the focus for a few seconds.

Edit your bookshelf

210

Spend some time this evening pruning your bookshelves to make room for new and enlightening books. Make a pile of unwanted titles to be taken to the thrift store (wise people do charity work) or to resell online (they are also frugal).

Also hook out books from your past that you would like to revisit and leave them by your bed for late-night perusal.

211 Control your finances

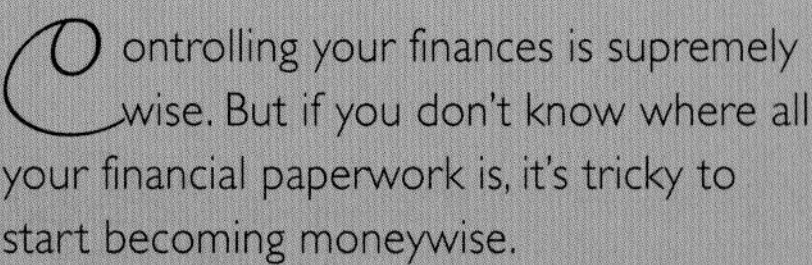

Controlling your finances is supremely wise. But if you don't know where all your financial paperwork is, it's tricky to start becoming moneywise.

Today, spend an hour gathering together all your bank and credit-card statements, receipts and check stubs. File like with like in order of date, graded into separate files or in a larger file with dividers. Make a pledge to file everything in the right place as it comes into your home. This will equip you to begin controlling your finances.

Wise tale: sage advice

212

When Patanjali, the ancient Indian sage, came to earth, he outlined grammar and ayurvedic healthcare. Then he codified yoga practices into an eight-stranded path. The first and second paths are a code for ethical living. The five don'ts *(yama)* are non-violence, truth, not stealing, celibacy or being faithful and lack of greed. The five dos *(niyama)* are cleanliness, contentment, perseverance, self-study and surrendering to God. Next come body postures *(asana)* and breath-control techniques *(pranayama)*. The final strands are: withdrawal of the senses *(pratyahara)*, concentration *(dharana)*, meditation *(dhyana)* and enlightenment *(samadhi)*.

Wisdom: *there are practical steps to follow on the path to self-knowledge, and we can take a lifetime over them if we wish.*

checklist 7 How did you do?

Whether you tried out several ideas this month or just one, you might like to reflect on what you chose to try and why, and if it worked for you.

1. How many activities did you try this month?

- 1–3 activities ☐
- 4–10 activities ☐
- 11–20 activities ☐
- 21–30 activities ☐

2. How many did you repeat several times in the month?

- 1–3 activities ☐
- 4–10 activities ☐
- 11–20 activities ☐
- 21–30 activities ☐

3. Which activities had a positive effect on your sense of innate wisdom this month?

Use the page opposite to make notes about what worked for you and what didn't.

Notes, jottings and thoughts

213 Talk to co-workers

Wise thought

SHARE THE JOY
Lend books that have inspired you in the past to your friends and family.

Instead of emailing today, stand up and walk to your co-worker's desk or office. This not only adds vital steps to your day, it establishes personal contacts that bond businesses and underpin future career opportunities; all adding to personal and corporate knowledge and wisdom. In one study, engaging in a mere ten minutes of conversation boosted intellectual capabilities as much as doing a jigsaw puzzle.

Try moving meditation

214

Taiwanese research has shown that the discipline of t'ai chi can boost the functioning of the cardio-respiratory system and microcirculation: both keep the brain working keenly.

This form of exercise also seems to increase strength, balance, flexibility and psychological wellbeing and to actually delay the decline of physical functioning as we age. Explore local options today and favor groups that sometimes practice outdoors.

215 Places to think

Wise thought

SWITCH OFF

For studying, choose a quiet, warm place where you won't be disturbed and switch off your phone.

Adopt a favorite spot outdoors where you can sit and meditate in peace. Look for a gnarled tree to rest your back against, a hill with a view, a secluded park bench or natural rock seat. Make this a destination to walk to when you need to escape the chaos of home or work, or when you need to puzzle over a problem.

So will I build my altar in the fields,
And the blue sky my fretted dome shall be...

Samuel Taylor Coleridge

Make eye contact

216

On your first journey out of the house this morning, try greeting a neighbor or perhaps the person who serves your coffee or sells you a train ticket.

If you're feeling intrepid, make eye contact with a complete stranger and give them a nice smile. It's this easy to start creating positive communities, but it needs a starting point and this is where you can come in. Research suggests that frequent social interaction can delay age-related memory loss.

217 Make connections

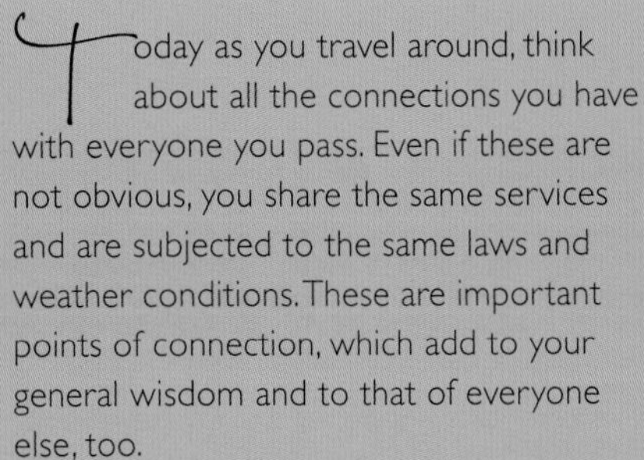

Today as you travel around, think about all the connections you have with everyone you pass. Even if these are not obvious, you share the same services and are subjected to the same laws and weather conditions. These are important points of connection, which add to your general wisdom and to that of everyone else, too.

All things are woven together and the common bond is sacred, and scarcely one thing is foreign to another, for they have been arranged together in their places and together make the same ordered Universe.

Marcus Aurelius

Be a tourist

218

Make plans to spend a day off or a weekend day as a tourist in your own home town. Visit the sites you've never had time to see and go to places you've neglected or forgotten about.

Read the town guides, take an open-top bus or guided tour of a historical building and have lunch in a tourist café. Seeing your world in such a new light refreshes your perceptions and adds depth and wisdom to your life in that place.

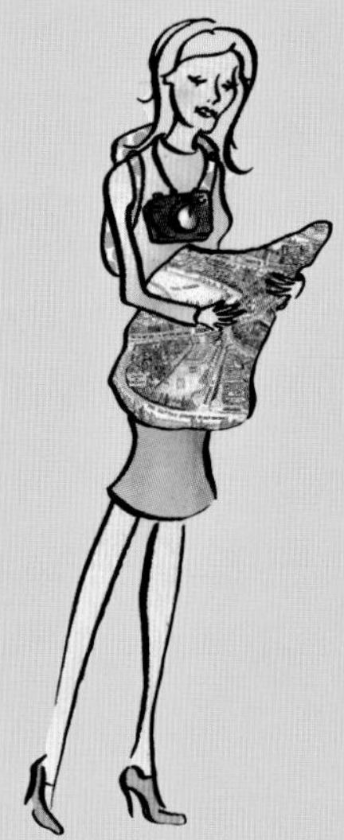

219 Make new friends

Today consider the people you encounter every day, but who you rarely acknowledge; perhaps the woman who serves you lunch or who swipes you in at the gym. How could you make their day less stressful? Do you ever say 'thank you' or crack a joke?

Make a start today. Notice whether you experience 'helper's high'; a feeling of elation followed by a sense of accomplishment. That's wisdom in action.

Adapt yourself to the environment in which your lot has been cast, and show true love to the fellow-mortals with whom destiny has surrounded you.

Marcus Aurelius

Try Cobbler Pose

220

This yoga posture ensures a good supply of blood to your pelvic region and keeps the hips and knees mobile, which helps you stay active and alert; all adding to your overall wisdom.

Sit with your buttocks touching a wall. Bend your knees, bring the soles of your feet together and clasp your toes with both hands, pulling your feet toward your groin (if this is tricky, wrap a scarf around your feet and pull on both ends to draw them in). Sit up straight and press your chest forward, using your arms as levers. Press your knees toward the ground. Hold for 30–60 seconds before stretching your legs.

221 Stick up your hand

Wise thought

HOW CAN YOU HELP?

Start easy by selling raffle tickets or attending a charity event.

People who volunteer report a more positive self-image and feelings of wellbeing, which seem to translate into a happier, less stressful, life. They also retain their mental acuity longer into old age. What can you sign up to today? Is your workplace involved in work in the community? If not, could you be the person who galvanizes a group of co-workers into action?

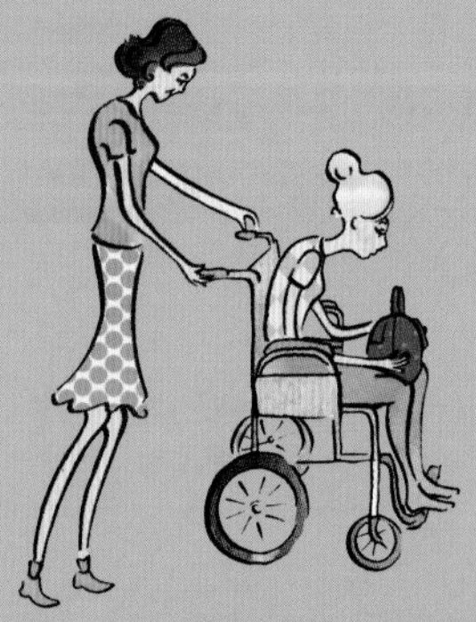

Speak without notes

222

Being able to speak in public or give a presentation without notes makes you seem wiser than perhaps you feel. It makes thoughts seem more heartfelt, too. First work on your subject closely, until you know it inside-out. Then boost your confidence with good preparation.

Write out a plan using bullet points (but don't write the speech out word for word). Group thoughts under headings, adding memorable phrases. Put images to each main thought, or think of the speech as a journey and visualize objects along the way. Link examples in threes, a storytelling technique that makes them easier to remember. Also use alliteration. Finally, practice the speech to yourself, out loud and to others (keep a crib sheet to hand containing the paragraph headings, but try not to look at it).

223 Buy a pedometer

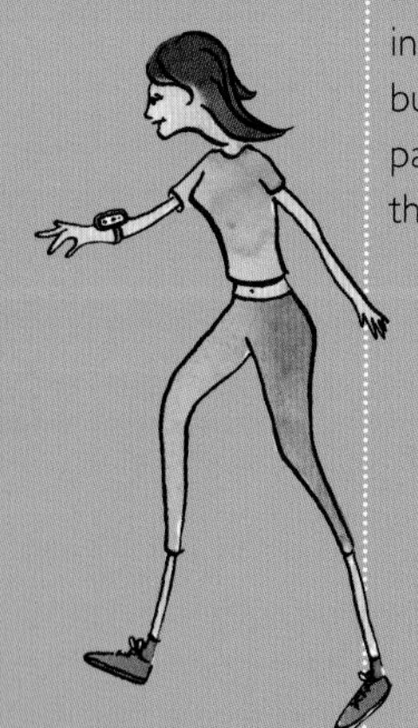

Walking is one of the best ways to boost mental alertness, honing your ability to make decisions, concentrate with focus and solve problems. You may notice results after only 15 minutes.

If you need added encouragement for increasing the amount of walking you do, buy a pedometer. It's magical to watch the paces mount up and a real incentive to go that extra mile.

In every walk with nature one receives far more than he seeks.

John Muir

Turn off your phone

224

Can you cope for a morning or afternoon, or even a whole day, without your phone? Studies suggest that electronic interruptions make us more distracted and therefore less productive at work. Try for at least part of today just to focus on the task in hand. Don't be in thrall to the electronic bleep.

Use sandalwood soap

225

Sandalwood is used in temples and for prayer beads and is sought after for its ability to encourage and support insightful meditation and prayer. Use pure sandalwood soap in your morning shower; look for quality soap imported from Mysore in India.

226 Eat together

If your household tends to eat at different times, make tonight's dinner a shared experience. Eating with others is associated with a widened vocabulary and raised school grades plus cultivation of communication and closeness. So it makes perfect sense for deepening family wisdom. If getting together in the week is too difficult, try weekends.

Think about practical issues that make eating together problematic. Do you need to leave your workplace on time, write a shopping list or perhaps create a food preparation and cooking rota? Most importantly, who gets to choose what you all eat?

A meditation notebook

227

Take a few minutes to record any unusual feelings you experience while you are meditating, good or bad, and any difficulties or distractions you notice. These may be repressed thoughts, images that disturb you, even laughter.

Be reassured that these experiences are common and evidence that the practice is touching you on a deep level.

228 Rest and relax

After a good meal, you are likely to feel sleepy as your body diverts attention to processing food rather than servicing the brain. So it's a good plan not to attempt very brain-taxing tasks for 30 minutes after eating.

Look at your journal and check what activities you have planned for post-mealtimes today. Can you rearrange your schedule to make use of the times when you are likely to feel more focused?

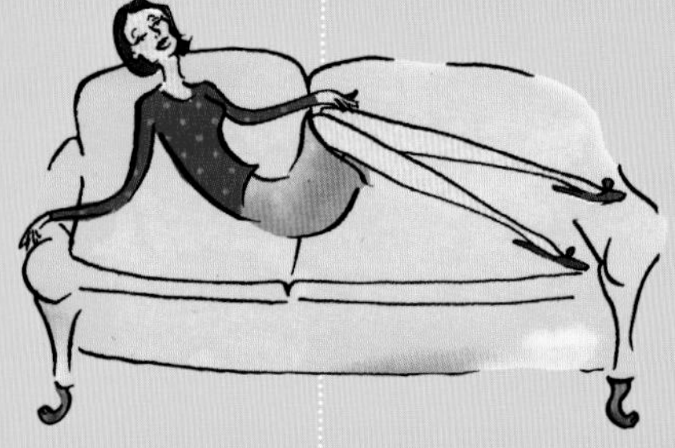

Celebrate culinary heritage

229

The diets that keep our bodies healthiest and minds functioning well have one thing in common; they are traditional. Think about the staple dishes from your family heritage, such as rice and peas, chicken soup, gumbo, sushi or dhal.

Today, try to eat the way your ancestors did, avoiding any processed or packaged goods that they might not recognize as food. Call your mother or grandmother for a recipe or invest in a cookbook.

Wise thought

WORLD TRADITIONS

If you don't have a food tradition of your own, adopt one. Choose from Mediterranean, Middle Eastern or Japanese cuisines, which all have well-known health benefits.

230 Stay at home

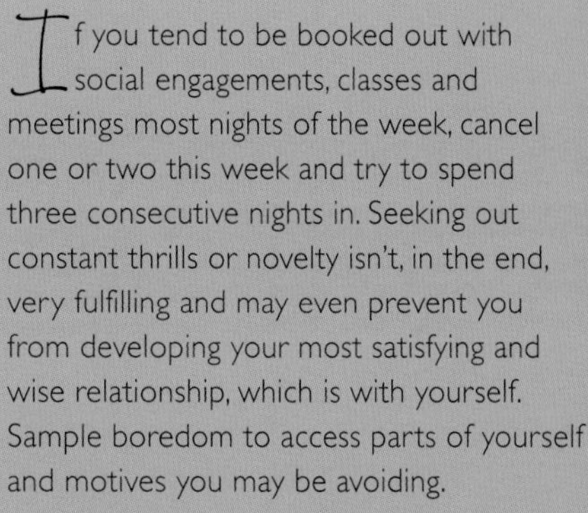

If you tend to be booked out with social engagements, classes and meetings most nights of the week, cancel one or two this week and try to spend three consecutive nights in. Seeking out constant thrills or novelty isn't, in the end, very fulfilling and may even prevent you from developing your most satisfying and wise relationship, which is with yourself. Sample boredom to access parts of yourself and motives you may be avoiding.

Without stirring abroad, one can know the whole world;
Without looking out of the window one can see the way of heaven. The further one goes the less one knows.

Lao-Tzu

Open your eyes

231

If you find yourself closing your eyes and becoming lost in thought when you practice an inward-looking form of exercise, such as yoga or qi gong, gently remind yourself to open your eyes and focus outside yourself. This will assist you in your search for insightfulness and contribute to your overall wise self.

If you need a physical focus, look in the direction of the tip of your nose in upward-looking poses, at your outstretched fingers in standing poses, at your toes in forward bends and toward your navel in inversions. This directs and engages your intelligence, making every movement better judged.

232 First priorities

In the following quotation from the great Chinese thinker Confucius, he asks us to connect what happens in our personal lives with what happens in the world. Look at how he guides us step-by-step through those connections. If you want to make a change to the world, try to follow this model:

To put the world right in order, we must first put the nation in order; to put the nation in order, we must first put the family in order; to put the family in order, we must first cultivate our personal life; we must first set our hearts right.

Confucius

The benefits of rapture

233

Try to do something today that makes you feel truly electrified. Why is this important for greater wisdom? It focuses you on the moment with such intensity that all preoccupations fade, leaving you with a clear sense of who you are right now. This helps to put worries into perspective and helps you to act with better judgment and more empathy.

An enchanted life has many moments when the heart is overwhelmed with beauty and the imagination is electrified by some haunting quality in the world or by a spirit or voice speaking from deep within a thing, a place or a person.

Thomas More

234 A night at the opera

Today book seats for the opera or a classical concert. Classical music tends to deal in bigger emotions, over a more sustained period of time, than the pop song and so can offer us a wider range of emotions and ideas to sample. In particular, surrendering yourself to the big themes offered in opera provides a cathartic experience that helps to dissipate difficult emotions.

To gain insight into the work before the big night, search the library or online for a précis of the opera's plot or a biography of the composer, but try to go without preconceptions.

Consider karma

235

The Sanskrit word *karma* means 'action' and describes the effects your thoughts or actions have on the future. Many people perceive the law of karma to be a fatalistic force that resigns them to whatever life throws their way. But karma is an empowering notion.

Today, think about how responding to whatever life throws at you in a positive way helps you to take control of a situation and prompts others to behave more positively, too. This sets up a circuit of positivity that benefits your future and everyone in it.

Our deeds determine us as much as we determine our deeds.

George Eliot

236 Read while awake

Though a great habit to get into, reading at bedtime can mean falling asleep over ideas and missing great chunks of plot. Today, try to read when your mind is fresh and your eyes are not tired. And try not to read lying down. Sitting with your back straight keeps the brain alert.

237 Find a poem

On the way home tonight be aware of the words all around you: on car number plates, advertizing hoardings and in newspapers. Choose words from these random writings that say something about your mental state today and use them to construct a short poem.

Candle-gazing

238

This exercise is thought to cleanse your eyes while boosting your concentration on a single point, which steadies and focuses the mind.

Sit comfortably and light a candle or night-light level with your eyes and about an arm's length away. Stare at the flame. Choose a single point, perhaps the edge of the blue of the flame, without blinking. Soften your gaze rather than staring. Do this until tears come. This is considered to be cleansing.

Now shut your eyes and recreate the image of the flame on the screen of your mind. Ignore the flashy optical show that results from looking at a bright light. Rather, recreate the light within yourself. This steers your mind toward single-pointed focus.

Folded eyes see brighter colours than the open ever do.

Elizabeth Barrett Browning

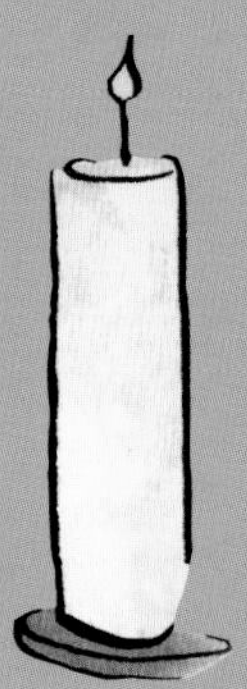

239 Wise-owl visualization

We consider owls wise in part because their huge eyes and their ability to turn their heads further gives them a perspective that is much wider than our own.

Why not help to break out of the limits of your regular vision with the following exercise? Sit quietly with your eyes open. Think about how you usually look and let your mind be distracted by the visual stimulus of all that is around you: light, colors, shapes and objects. See how your mind follows these into trails of distracting thoughts. Now close your eyes to these delusions and find your real sight, or 'insight', which is stable and unchanging. Try to use this wiser vision to inform and influence your dealings with the world tomorrow.

Bedtime breathing

240

When you have greater control over your breath you are one step nearer to wise self-realization, teach the practitioners of yoga.

Sit quietly tonight and watch your breathing. Once you feel calm, exhale completely, then breathe in one-third of the way and hold the breath briefly. Breathe in again until your lungs are two-thirds full, then hold your breath again. Finally top up the air until your lungs are completely full; right up to your shoulders. Hold again briefly before exhaling smoothly and fully. Repeat this five times, visualizing yourself filling an empty jar.

Wise thought

FILTER

Don't forget to close your mouth when breathing in, to filter impurities out of the incoming air.

241 Enjoy a lie-in

Treat yourself to an extra half hour in bed this morning, if you can. Don't think of this as idling. To nurture creative thinking, the imagination needs regular periods of time off, when it has free rein to ponder 'what-if' scenarios.

In a world of wall-to-wall entertainment and long work hours, many of us don't have such empty times. Take advantage of the down-time today by trying to stay aware as you daydream. Notice interesting ideas or apparently unconnected notions suddenly linking together. This is a sign of an especially creative thinker.

Wise tale: the sage owl

242

Scholar, night-time warrior and prophesying messenger, the owl is a powerful symbol of wisdom in many traditions. Athene, Greek goddess of wisdom, emerged, says Hesiod, at her birth 'owl-eyed' and wears on her shield the image of an owl's head. Athene is also goddess of war, and the owl's penetrative sight, three-dimensional hearing and silent flight makes it a great warrior. This creature of the night can see the truth in darkness and in detail. The owl has access to supernatural truth, too, say legends; the secret knowledge of the spirit world is hers, equipping her with great foresight.

Wisdom: *which of the owl's reputed or actual qualities could enrich your life today: foresight, sensitivity to sound or silent movement? Make this wise bird your special talisman.*

checklist 8 How did you do?

Whether you tried out several ideas this month or just one, you might like to reflect on what you chose to try and why, and if it worked for you.

1. How many activities did you try this month?

- 1–3 activities ☐
- 4–10 activities ☐
- 11–20 activities ☐
- 21–30 activities ☐

2. How many did you repeat several times in the month?

- 1–3 activities ☐
- 4–10 activities ☐
- 11–20 activities ☐
- 21–30 activities ☐

3. Which activities had a positive effect on your sense of innate wisdom this month?

Use the page opposite to make notes about what worked for you and what didn't.

Notes, jottings and thoughts

243 Daybreak thanksgiving

On waking this morning, give thanks for all the good things you have in your life that contribute to your life-wisdom. For the people who support you, the time to think, the thoughts that inspire you and the opportunity to learn. Don't forget to honor all the little things that make your life pleasurable, too. This could be the butter in your morning pastry, the grip on your yoga mat, the luxurious feel of cashmere socks. Wisdom means sustaining a dual awareness, of the big picture and the little details.

The best things in life are nearest: breath in your nostrils, light in your eyes, flowers at your feet, duties at your hand, the path of right just before you.

Robert Louis Stevenson

Join a choir

244

If you enjoy singing to yourself around the home, take the plunge and join a local choir. Singing has proven benefits for the respiratory and circulatory systems, boosting the flow of blood and oxygen to the brain, which promotes clear thinking.

Singing in choirs also stimulates memory skills and involves socializing, helping to develop self-esteem and build a social support network. Both the latter are associated with keeping the brain acting youthful as we age.

245 Light a candle

Silent reflection and quiet prayer can deepen understanding or offer you insight in times of trouble. Try this out by lighting a nightlight or votive candle tonight for a loved one in distress or someone close to you who has died.

Meditate on that person, sending them good thoughts and love or giving thanks for their life. Don't expect supernatural healing or dramatic transformation; prayer is not about delivering solutions. Instead, ask for wisdom and the ability to trust and seek truth. Doing this in a place of worship may give you more powerful effects.

Better to light a candle than to curse the darkness.

Chinese proverb

Practice persistence

246

Look up the word 'persistence' in a dictionary. Spend some time today thinking about how you could apply some of these qualities to your own life; your work, your relationships and your free time.

Think of a hobby, project or New Year's resolution you began with enthusiasm then later abandoned. What would make you apply yourself with more determination next time round? Knowledge, support, the involvement of friends or family? Make a list in your journal.

This is the highest wisdom that I own; freedom and life are earned by those alone who conquer them each day anew.

Goethe

247 Write your own obituary

Writing your own obituary sounds like a depressing exercise, but it can actually be a wise and uplifting exercise, galvanizing us into taking positive action for the future.

Contemplating death is a key to attaining greater wisdom in many religious traditions. Start by making a detailed timeline of all the significant events in your life. Put dates to them. How would outsiders view these achievements? Write an account based on your timeline using the third person ('she/he did this') as if today were the last day of your life. Make up quotations from people about your qualities. How does your life read? Are you ready to finish it there? Now list all the things you will achieve before your real obituary hits the newsdesk.

Quieten your thoughts

248

If your mind disturbs you this evening with its constant chatter, imagine you have a volume dial that you can use to turn it down at will.

It might be disconcerting to turn it down to zero at first, so just take it halfway to start with. You will find that the voices are whispers rather than deafening shouts.

249 Sip ginger tea

Wise thought

FRESH LEMON

For extra zest, or if you have a cold, add the juice of half a freshly squeezed lemon to your ginger tea.

Ginger root contains oils that are shown to boost the circulatory and respiratory systems, providing just the kick you need at the start of the day to get your brain in gear. Try substituting ginger tea for coffee if you enjoy the mental stimulation a shot of caffeine gives but dislike its jittery side-effects.

Simply grate 12 mm (½ in) of fresh ginger root into a mug and pour over just-boiled water. Steep for ten minutes then sweeten with honey.

Morning exercise

250

Try to get into the habit of taking some sort of exercise in the mornings. A study found that this boosted mood by an average of 30 per cent. Starting the day in a positive mood makes it more likely that you will be clear-thinking, able to call up the resources to tackle problems, and get on well with co-workers.

An early-morning walk is a blessing for the whole day.

Henry David Thoreau

Instant wisdom

BREAK IT UP

If you can't fit in your daily requirement of 30 minutes' exercise in the morning, break it down into two 15-minute sessions.

251 Work that brain

Instant wisdom

PUSH YOURSELF
Using your brain increases its potential: start *War and Peace*, do a crossword or play chess today.

On your morning commute today or during a break, complete a sudoku puzzle. To keep brain function acute, we need to keep using it.

Filling in sudoku squares exercises the brain's neural pathways involved in associative memory, or finding patterns from partial clues. This helps us to exercise our powers of guesswork and to discern feelings of right and wrong. In daily life, it helps us to make connections between names and faces.

Start saying grace

252

Before you eat tonight, give thanks for your food, and to all those involved in getting it to your plate. If you don't feel comfortable thanking God, praise Mother Nature or the earth for their gifts.

If this feels too much, sit in silence and think about the interdependence of the world of animals, plants and people, and about the debt we owe others for our food. Being meditative before meals and during them is thought, in many traditions, to show our innate human intellect. It sets us apart from the animals.

Instant wisdom

SHOW RESPECT
To show respect for your food, eat at a table with a knife and fork rather than grazing in front of the TV.

253 Learning from adversity

Think about what happened to you yesterday. What didn't go according to plan? What mistakes did you make? Try to drown out any feelings of humiliation or despondency by making a list of what you could do differently next time. What could you do to avoid that situation or improve performance? Take heart; if you hadn't made that mistake, you wouldn't now have that insight. The wise give thanks for their mistakes and move on, enlightened.

Well – life is just the same as learning to swim! Do not be afraid of making mistakes, for there is no other way of learning how to live!

Alfred Adler

Play energizing music

254

Put on a rousing tune as you get ready for work this morning. This will help to dissipate torpor and galvanize you into action; a wise move. Wagner's 'Ride of the Valkyries' is excellent, as is Rossini's 'William Tell Overture'.

Stop Googling

255

Today try to do something bigger than bite-sized. Instead of Googling little snippets of information, try to read a sizeable chunk of a book. Replace Wikipedia with an acclaimed author's take on a subject and immerse yourself in one person's view of the world.

256 Know when to speak

'Tis better to be silent and be thought a fool, than to speak and remove all doubt.

Abraham Lincoln (attributed)

In new or stressful situations some of us have the urge to fill silent gaps with chatter. Today, try to quell this urge. If you've got nothing interesting to contribute, just listen to others for a while. If you're asked a question and don't know the answer, don't get flustered; simply say you don't know in the simplest words, with a smile.

In interview situations, ask your interviewer to rephrase the question so that you have time to think. Turn down any judgmental internal voices telling that you you're being dumb. If it helps, think of these internal chatterers as naughty monkeys and give them a good telling off (or bananas to keep their mouths full!).

Try Janu Sirsasana

257

This posture folds you forward, closing down the parts of the body with which we engage with the world: the eyes, mouth and hands, making us wiser individuals.

Sit in Dandasana (see Day 37, page 47). Have a firm bolster or cushion ready. Fold your left leg to the side and back, placing the sole against the top of the thigh or groin. Sit up tall. Breathing out, pivot forward from your hips, keeping the front of your body extended and without curving the upper back. If you can manage it, clasp your outstretched toes, or just recline onto the cushion, keeping your hands on the floor on either side of your legs. Hold for up to a minute, then repeat on the other leg.

258 Morning breath

Bring together two breathing techniques. Breathe in gradually, pausing briefly before filling your lungs a third full, then two-thirds, then to the brim. Now breathe out in three sections. As you practice, try to keep your mind focused on the movement of air and let this override other thoughts; this helps to calm your mind and focus your thoughts. Notice how long the beneficial effects last this morning.

When the breath wanders the mind also is unsteady. But when the breath is calmed the mind too will be still, and the yogi achieves long life. Therefore, one should learn to control the breath.

Hatha Yoga Pradipika

Ditch the baggage

259

When dressing this morning and packing your bag for work or study, try to pare what you take down to a minimum, for it's wise to live simply. Put the absolute essentials for the day to one side. Now assess the also-rans. Remove the comfort blankets; that just-in-case cardigan, scarf or extra pair of shoes. Look, too, at the electronic gizmos and try to do without one or two.

Traveling light makes your day's journey less stressful on your back and you will feel more spontaneous. You are now free to improvise and think on your feet; to make do and use your nouse. And that makes you a more engaged and engaging person.

260 Recognize a guru

We all need direction to uncover our spiritual nature. You might find that guidance in a yoga teacher, a priest or with a philosopher.

So if you find inspiration in someone's words or in a book, pursue it further by attending more of their classes or services and reading more of their books.

When the student is ready, the Master appears.

Buddhist proverb

Make something to wear

261

Just 30 years ago, most women knew how to sew, knit or crochet an item of clothing. Unfortunately, many of us have lost this knowledge. Call an older relative who remembers how and ask her for a lesson tonight, or look for a class in creative recycling of clothes. Plenty of stylish online sites offer patterns for easy dresses and skirts. Surprise yourself with your skills!

Instant wisdom

TRANSFORMATION
Transform an off-the-rack garment by changing the buttons for beautiful hand-crafted or vintage versions.

262 Energy focus

When you lack energy or feel you are overtaxed by work, try this yogic energy-raising technique with a friend. Sit with knees apart and buttocks resting on your heels, then gradually lower your upper body forward so your forehead rests on the floor or on a firm cushion. Rest your arms comfortably in front of your head.

Ask your friend to kneel behind you and place her palms gently on your sacrum (bony area at the base of your spine), one hand on each side of your spine. Now imagine breathing into her palms for two to three minutes and notice how, after a few breaths, you can feel this area 'moving'. This should help you to access the well of energy and innate wisdom which yogis believe lies at the base of the spine. Swap places and repeat on your partner's sacrum.

Go in for sport

263

A sport with rules that allow you to be bold, take chances and succeed or fail with a team is good for the brain as well as the body. Research has found that it activates parts of the brain linked with planning and controlling and it also boosts language skills.

Watching sports has similarly beneficial effects on language skills and understanding because it changes the neural networks that support comprehension. Watch your team with fellow fans: this has been shown to make for better peer relationships and boost self-esteem.

A strong body makes the mind strong.

Thomas Jefferson

264 Plan a vacation

Instant wisdom

BOOK NOW

If you find it hard to take your yearly holiday allowance, today block out two weeks next summer and inform your boss that you've booked the time off. Telling someone important makes it more attainable.

People who take frequent vacations benefit their mental health and suffer from less stress, depression and tiredness. Vacations are insightful because you're more likely to go with the flow and try new activities, which can boost self-confidence and deepen relationships. Holidays away from home also give you the time and distance required to reassess where you are going in your life.

Learn about philanthropy

265

It's a long word! Do you know any philanthropists? Think about those who give without being financially wealthy. What do these wise individuals donate instead of their money? What is it that sets their life apart from yours?

Read a book on the life of a well-known philanthropist to find out what makes such generous people tick and how their backgrounds or childhood experiences formed their giving outlook. The lives of Benjamin Franklin and George Peabody make good reading.

If you want to lift yourself up, lift up someone else.

Booker T Washington

266 Breathe out fully

If you take long, deep in-breaths you ensure that your brain has all the oxygen it needs to function well. But many of us find it difficult to breathe in smoothly and deeply. The reason can be simple; you may not be exhaling fully, making it tricky to take a deep in-breath.

Try this exercise. Take a full breath in and exhale one-third of the way, pause briefly, then exhale further. Pause again, then totally empty your lungs; you might like to puff out the last bit. Now enjoy taking a long, deep in-breath, visualizing all that vitalizing oxygen rejuvenating every system in your body.

Do something new

267

Today do something you've never done before. Sleep on the 'wrong' side of the bed, listen to a new radio station or try eating a new vegetable. If your usual exercise class fails to present you with challenges, try a new form, particularly one that uses bands, balls or other 'props'. If you have a daily yoga practice, shake up your expectations by performing the poses in a different order or by practicing postures you tend to avoid.

Novelty poses challenges to our preconceptions and provokes new, often unexpected, emotional responses. This keeps the brain active and alert and makes you a more engaging, yet humble, person.

268 Learn a poem

Older generations were expected to rote-learn poetry. Some people might not always have enjoyed it, but as a result they have a rich seam of deep thoughts at their disposal.

Poetry is known to be good for the brain because it short-circuits thoughts and uses juxtaposition to subvert your perception of the meanings of words. Try to learn a poem today. Look at *Pied Beauty* by Gerald Manley Hopkins, *Twelve Songs IX* by W H Auden or *The Listeners* by Walter de la Mare.

Try drawing the body

269

Join a life-drawing class to understand more about how the human body moves and to counteract any expectations we have about our bodies, formed by years looking at retouched and surgically sculpted bodies in magazines.

Having permission to look allows us to learn and accept, as does engaging with these real bodies by spending time trying to turn three-dimensional shapes into drawn lines. This insight allows us to deepen our personal wisdom.

Pleasure can be supported by an illusion; but happiness rests upon truth.

Sébastien-Roch Nicolas De Chamfort

270 Bedtime thought

How do we find a wise path through life? By quietening the ego and all that it gets involved in: pride, temptation, deception, manipulation and dishonesty. This is a lifelong challenge, but start tonight by sitting in silence and trying to catch the gap between your thoughts. In this elusive space is wisdom, but catching it is as tricky as catching a wave when you begin to surf. Keep paddling!

In the attitude of silence the soul finds the path in a clearer light, and what is elusive and deceptive resolves itself into crystal clearness. Our life is a long and arduous quest after Truth.

Mahatma Gandhi

Make a berry breakfast

271

Add a medley of berries to your morning muesli. Blueberries, bilberries, blackcurrants and lingonberries are high in flavonoids, which are plant pigments that help mop up the free-radicals that damage body cells. Flavonoids may inhibit some of the decline in cognitive function that happens naturally as we age, keeping us feeling and acting intelligent.

Wise thought

YEAR-ROUND GOODNESS

Buy berries frozen to enjoy year-round. In studies, frozen berries contained as much of the cell-protecting flavonoid quercetin as the freshly picked fruit.

272 Keep silence

Instant wisdom

SILENCE AND WISDOM

To gain insight into why silence brings us closer to wisdom, read *A Book of Silence* by Sara Maitland; an account of her attempt to live a significant part of her life in silence.

After closing your door on the world today, try to spend at least an hour in complete silence. Turn off your phones, the radio, TV and music. Keep away from conversation. Simply engage in light household tasks, such as cooking, washing up, chopping firewood or knitting.

You will notice how loud your inner voice is. But if you practice this yogic technique known as *mouna* regularly, this voice, too, will calm after a few weeks, delivering you to a place of peace. Why does this make you a wiser person? People who spend time in silence say that it makes us more honest, deep-thinking and attentive to others and the natural world.

Wise tale: wilderness days

273

For 40 days and 40 nights, Christ retreated into the wilderness to fast and reflect. During this time he was assaulted by wild animals and experienced temptation in many forms. Satan goaded him to prove his divinity: 'Turn stones into bread,' he urged. 'Throw yourself from this great height to see if angels will catch you.' Then Satan revealed all the glittering kingdoms that could be Christ's if he would worship a false God. Each time Jesus kept the faith, remembering God's command to worship only him and his word. At the end of his ordeal, angels came to soothe him.

Wisdom: *test your beliefs and compare them to see how they, and you, stand up in times of doubt or hardship.*

checklist 9 How did you do?

Whether you tried out several ideas this month or just one, you might like to reflect on what you chose to try and why, and if it worked for you.

1. How many activities did you try this month?

- 1–3 activities ☐
- 4–10 activities ☐
- 11–20 activities ☐
- 21–31 activities ☐

2. How many did you repeat several times in the month?

- 1–3 activities ☐
- 4–10 activities ☐
- 11–20 activities ☐
- 21–31 activities ☐

3. Which activities had a positive effect on your sense of innate wisdom this month?

Use the page opposite to make notes about what worked for you and what didn't.

Notes, jottings and thoughts

274 Time for you

Make room for 'me-time' today. You might decide to take a long bath, join a meditation class or go for a swim. As you enter the water or exercise studio, leave other thoughts and concerns at the door. If you have more time, why not go for a long walk in the wilderness by yourself?

This time is for you, not for your worries, schedule demands or other people's concerns. It can help to breathe in deeply, then breathe out, imagining worries detaching themselves from you like leaves from a tree on a windy day. Repeat a few times until you feel lighter and more 'me-centered'.

Honor your mouth

275

If your body is a temple, then your mouth is its front door. Make sure today that everything that passes over the threshold is worthy and will contribute to your inner wisdom.

That means food and drink which makes your body feel energized, strong and clean. Processed foods and those loaded with sugar or salt usually don't fit the bill.

276 Daisy meditation

If you feel assaulted by stress or others' demands today, remove yourself from the situation and sit somewhere quiet. Close your eyes and visualize a daisy. See its outspread petals and yellow center open to the sun to absorb life-giving rays and to attract the attention of bees and other insects. Now visualize the sun fading and dawn setting in. As the sky reddens and the sun sinks visualize the daisy closing in on itself and safely withdrawing its petals to allow its 'day's eye' to rest.

Why should a man's mind have been thrown into such close, sad, sensational, inexplicable relations with such a precarious object as his body?

Thomas Hardy

Have a laugh

277

Don't take yourself too seriously today; it's far wiser to have a good laugh. Make up 'knock-knock' jokes over the breakfast table, crack a topical joke with co-workers, confide in a friend about something silly from your past.

Laughter stimulates many areas of the brain, including those connected with rational analysis, social and emotional responses, sensory processing and motor activity. It reduces levels of stress hormones and boosts the immune system, too, while giving you a cardiovascular workout.

278

We shall overcome

Today, contemplate these words of wisdom from the medieval mystic Julian of Norwich. It is unrealistic, she tells us, to expect to find freedom from storms, overwork or illness. What we should keep in mind, she says, is that we are stronger than these troubles, and are wise enough to overcome them.

He said not 'Thou shalt not be tempested, thou shalt not be travailed, thou shalt not be dis-eased,' but he said, 'Thou shalt not be overcome.'

Julian of Norwich

Consider yourself

279

Observe your reactions today. You will be able to notice your responses to situations and people as they occur, and then select the most appropriate for the situation. This doesn't mean not reacting.

Once you have considered the options and consequences, feel free to flame up with anger, to scold or scream. But you will find more often that your wisdom will instruct you not to.

280 Zip yourself up

Instant wisdom

JUST SAY 'NO'
Have the courage to say 'no thanks' today if you feel overburdened.

If you have to step into a stressful situation today, such as giving a talk or a meeting with your boss, use this energy technique to protect your sense of yourself and your belief in your inner wisdom.

Think back to a time when you felt positive, clever and empowered. Now place your right hand at your pubic bone and, breathing in, draw your fingers up the center of your body to your lips, as if you are pulling up a zip. Repeat this three times. Repeat an affirmation to yourself or out loud if it helps, such as 'I know I can do this' or 'I have all the knowledge I need to convince anyone.'

Thought for today

281

If your good intentions waver when you are faced with temptation, maybe between the chocolate cake and the apple or the bar and the gym, you need to have ammunition at hand.

Arm yourself today by memorizing the following wise words from The Buddha, which emphasize the importance of a healthy way of life in keeping the mind functioning with precision and discernment:

To keep the body in good health is a duty... otherwise we shall not be able to keep our mind strong and clear.

The Buddha

282 Walking with meaning

When repeated with intent as you walk, the words 'Lord, have mercy' from the Jesus Prayer are thought to still the emotions while strengthening the heart, or life force.

Use them as a breath meditation when you take a walk this lunchtime, breathing in with the first word and out with the second phrase. Individuals from many faiths and denominations have found these words highly effective.

Loaves and lilies

283

Your journey into wisdom should not be one of deprivation, and you should nurture yourself particularly well if you find any of the tasks emotionally draining. We can't live on loaves alone, says the proverb; the soul needs sustenance, too.

One of the best ways to feed the soul is by surrounding yourself with objects of beauty. So as well as feeding body and mind today, feed your spirit by buying a bunch of seasonal flowers or a flower in a pot.

If you have two loaves of bread, sell one and buy a lily.

Chinese proverb

284 Learn a language

To keep your brain on its toes, learn a language. Acquiring a new skill really does strengthen the connections between the synapses in the brain.

To keep up your motivation find a class that's easy to get to, maybe near work at lunchtime, and choose a language that you might use on vacation or at work.

285

Laugh yourself clean

As you shower this morning, start forming a joke in your head, bearing the following quotation in mind:

What soap is to the body, laughter is to the soul.

Yiddish proverb

286

Make tilleuil tea

Keep a box of tilleuil (linden or lime flower) teabags at home or work to sip in the morning and when you feel frazzled. This herb seems to rebalance the brain and emotions, relieving tension and feelings of panic and calming the mind.

287 Write your life story

We all have a work of fiction inside us. Start yours today by writing your autobiography. First map out the events over twelve chapters; they don't have to bring you right up to the present and they don't have to be chronological. Play with contrasting events or even work backward. Don't start writing until you are happy with this structure, and when you do, bear in mind these wise words:

Works of imagination should be written in very plain language; the more purely imaginative they are the more necessary it is to be plain.

Samuel Taylor Coleridge

Float away

288

Book a supremely calming session in a flotation tank; this is a sensory-deprivation experience in which you float weightlessly in a darkened room in water made buoyant with Epsom salts.

Therapists say that the sensory deprivation not only switches off stress responses, it helps to rebalance the right and left sides of the body and brain, leading to increased creativity and problem-solving skills. It also helps you to see situations and relationships with more clarity and insight.

289 Join a comedy class

You can learn how to laugh at yourself and the society you live in by signing up for an evening class in stand-up comedy. Tutors help you to express your unique take on the world and tap in to your innate motivation.

As well as gaining a greater understanding of who you are, stand-up classes are great for boosting self-esteem, public-speaking skills, the ability to engage with an audience and the art of the quick-thinking riposte.

Visit a graveyard

290

Put your life into perspective by taking a walk through a graveyard. After reading the names and dates and imagining the family stories of the people involved, simply sit on a bench and try to contemplate your own death.

Contemplating death every day is not morbid, but a time-honored way to become more thankful about everyday treasures and to live every moment to the full.

Do not fear death so much, but rather the inadequate life.

Bertolt Brecht

291 Talk to a child

Have a conversation today with a child who is under six years old. Ask them about life's most profound queries: what happens when we die, how can we be happier or about the nature of love. Be prepared to hear great truths and experience wide-ranging discussions that don't adhere to the norms and taboos of adult conversation.

Concentration mudra

292

A *mudra* is a hand gesture that is used in yoga and the concentration mudra is thought to increase the powers of concentration and stimulate your memory.

Join together the tips of the fingers of both hands in front of you, fingers pointing upward. Keep the digits straight and press the tips into each other firmly for up to a minute, with your wrists apart. Breathe slowly and deeply as you hold this hand position and look upward (without lifting your chin).

293 Innocence and experience

Read two short, simple poems by William Blake from his collection *Songs of Innocence and Experience*. The original book features etchings by the author that add to the thoughts explored.

First read the poem of innocence 'The Lamb', and think about its child narrator and his belief in God. Now read its companion poem, written from the standpoint of experience, 'The Tyger'. What has knowledge taught this narrator? And which viewpoint does the poet espouse?

Think about innocence

294

Think back to when you were a child. What beliefs did you have which today you would cast aside as silly? Perhaps you talked to an invisible friend, wrote notes to the Tooth Fairy or cried because of the monsters under the bed. What did it feel like? Where did that innate imagination go? Dip inside your imagination today and dredge up your beliefs by making up a fairy story or inventing a creation myth. How do you think the world came into being?

...each child has its fairy godmother in its own soul.

Francis Thompson

295 Unattached yoga

Watch how your senses draw your mind into a flustered state while you hold a yoga pose. Are you thinking about not wobbling or collapsing, when you can come out, or how much the backs of your legs hurt?

Draw your mind away from these disruptive distractions by focusing on the pose itself. This is a form of *pratyahara*, or withdrawing from your senses, and is a wiser way of approaching yoga practice.

Do a jigsaw

296

Become absorbed in an enthralling puzzle tonight instead of watching TV or gossiping on the phone. Choose a fiddly jigsaw puzzle featuring expanses of sky or sea. Set it out where it won't be disturbed, so you can return to it over days, or even weeks.

As you fiddle with the pieces let the puzzling distract you from other thoughts. And give grateful thanks for your brain. Even the most powerful computers can't do jigsaw puzzles as they are stumped by the sheer number of possible placements for each piece.

297 Cook with rosemary

The herb rosemary has long been used to strengthen the memory as it stimulates blood flow to the brain. It's also known for its uplifting properties, which can invigorate the system and raise the spirits. Spike fresh florets into lamb before roasting, add to vegetables before baking, knead into bread dough and add to marinades.

298 Learn a prayer

If you have no holy words in your head how can you start praying? Today learn one prayer from your own tradition or some words that speak to you. Those that ask for blessing or guidance, or which give thanks, are a good place to start.

A new dawn

299

Whatever you experience today, the frustrations, loss of concentration or good intentions, and lack of time or headspace, remember that tomorrow you can start afresh on your journey to greater wisdom. Before you go to sleep, read the quotation below and conjure up in your mind's eye the hopeful image of a summer's day breaking with its wide pink sunrise, suggesting boundless opportunities to come. Good night!

After winter comes the summer.
After night comes the dawn.
And after
every storm, there comes clear,
open skies.'

Samuel Rutherford

300 Withdrawing the senses

The yoga practice of *pratyahara* involves drawing your attention and energy in from the senses. Do this as you lie in bed. Listen to everything your ears are picking up. Imagine drawing your sense of hearing inside, so noises are less distracting. Now think about your eyes and draw your sense of sight within, so even if your eyes are open you see less. Do the same with your mouth and sense of taste, then your nose and sense of smell. Finally imagine all the sense receptors on your skin. Draw them inward so your body is less assaulted by touch. Drift off to sleep in this cocoon.

The senses deceive from time to time, and it is prudent never to trust wholly those who have deceived us even once.

René Descartes

Try Viparita Karani

301

The recuperative yoga pose, Viparita Karani, rests the heart and lungs and helps to relax the senses.

Place a firm bolster or some yoga blocks covered with a folded blanket beside a wall. Sit on the support side-on, with one hip and shoulder touching the wall. Now swivel around to take your legs up the wall and lower your back to the floor. Lie down comfortably with your arms away from your sides, palms up, and straighten your legs up the wall as much as possible. Relax here for three to five minutes with your eyes closed.

To come down, bend your knees, press the soles of your feet into the wall and carefully lower your buttocks to the floor.

302 Foot massage

Before bed tonight, massage warm oil into the soles of your feet. Either do it yourself or ask someone else to do it for you. In ayurvedic medicine this is thought to encourage peaceful sleep (essential if your brain is to perform well tomorrow). It doesn't matter what oil you use, though in India colorless sesame oil is recommended. Warm the oil by standing the bottle in a bowl of hot water for a few minutes before starting the massage.

The strokes don't matter either; just do whatever feels comforting, using long, stroking movements to start, moving on to deep knuckling or thumb-pressure movements and ending with more smooth gliding. To safeguard your sheets, put on clean cotton socks before slipping into bed.

Wise tale: Plato's cave

303

The Greek philosopher Plato tells us, in *The Republic*, of a cave deep within the rocks. Here, in the dark, sit a row of people chained to seats facing the back wall. They watch shadows cast against the cave's back wall when puppeteers pass objects behind them, lit by diffused sunlight and a fire. The people give names to these shadow animals and plants, believing they are real. This is the closest they ever get to reality; at third hand, interpreted by the puppeteers, then cast by shadows.

Wisdom: *are we content to rely on other people's interpretations of truth? How might we free ourselves, turn to see the objects and eventually leave the cave to experience life?*

checklist 10 How did you do?

Whether you tried out several ideas this month or just one, you might like to reflect on what you chose to try and why, and if it worked for you.

1. How many activities did you try this month?

- 1–3 activities ☐
- 4–10 activities ☐
- 11–20 activities ☐
- 21–30 activities ☐

2. How many did you repeat several times in the month?

- 1–3 activities ☐
- 4–10 activities ☐
- 11–20 activities ☐
- 21–30 activities ☐

3. Which activities had a positive effect on your sense of innate wisdom this month?

Use the page opposite to make notes about what worked for you and what didn't.

Notes, jottings and thoughts

304 Sit in stillness

From today, try to sit in stillness on the floor, with your back straight, for at least ten minutes in the morning before eating or drinking. How does this enhance wisdom? Yogis believe that in a good sitting position the body can be perfectly balanced and is at rest. This frees the diaphragm to breathe easily and the brain to achieve alertness and clear-thinking.

The ultimate sitting pose is Lotus Pose, the most stable seated position in yoga. Sit with your legs crossed. Lift your right leg and place the top of your foot on your left thigh, touching your abdomen, sole facing upward. Stop if you feel any tenderness or pain in your knee. Practice this, alternating legs, until it feels comfortable. Once one foot is comfortable on the opposite thigh, guide the other foot forward and up onto your other thigh. Rest your hands on your knees.

Be a mentor

305

Is there a mentoring scheme within your company or community? Why not step up and volunteer. Some schemes pair volunteers up with people who are socially isolated or excluded because of health issues, to help them access facilities or get together with peers.

Other schemes are more work-based, aiming to offer young people a foot on a ladder, a window on the world of work or simply a friend who will support and speak up for them. Research shows that both sides gain in self-confidence and motivation.

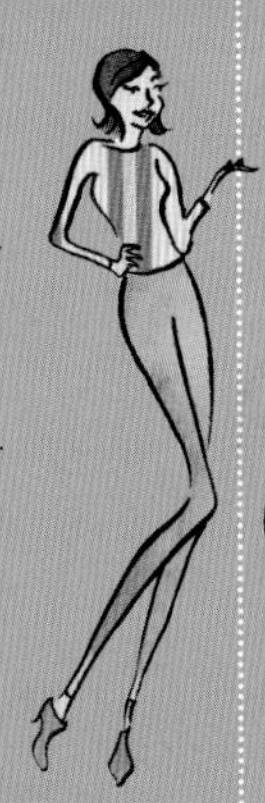

306 Fiddle with beads

Instant wisdom

DISTRACTION

If you are trying to give up smoking, drinking or snacking, worry beads offer the hands a helpful distraction activity.

If you find it difficult to sit in stillness to meditate, try using some prayer or worry beads. As you sit, hold the beads in your right hand and move one bead at a time with your thumb.

Coordinate the movements with your breathing: move the bead as you exhale, then pause at the space between the beads and enjoy the silence that comes at the end of an out-breath. Inhaling, lift your thumb onto the next bead and move it at the same time as the exhalation.

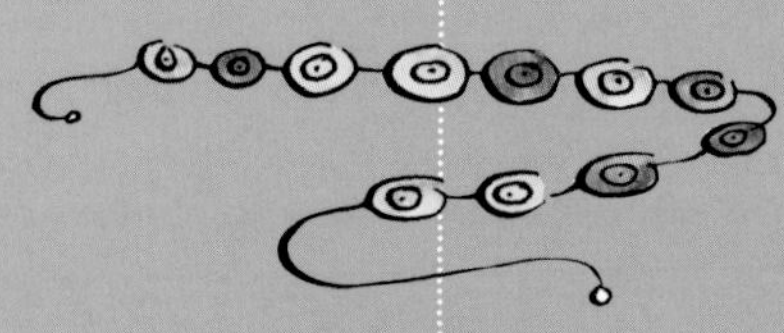

Clear your thinking

307

This energy technique helps you to start the day with a clear mind and focused concentration.

Find the gap in the center of both your collar bones with your index fingers. Move your fingers down about 2.5 cm (1 in) and out to each side. You should find a slight dip here; one on each side. Massage into the dips, or tap them with your fingers for about 20 seconds. If you don't feel any different, cross your hands and repeat with opposite fingers. Repeat whenever you switch off mentally during the day.

Life is a train of moods like a string of beads; and as we pass through them they prove to be many colored lenses, which paint the world their own hue, and each shows us only what lies in its own focus.

Ralph Waldo Emerson

308 Think from the heart

Educating the mind without educating the heart is no education at all.
Aristotle

When you have to answer a question today or make a tough decision, ask yourself what your wise heart would answer before speaking. If it helps, try this visualization before responding:

Close your eyes and conjure up an image of your heart. Watch it beating with vitality. Now imagine looking inside. There, in the center is a tiny pinprick of light. In many traditions this is thought to be a spark of divine essence. As you breathe in, visualize your breath fanning this flame, causing it to burn brighter. Do this for a few breaths, until the flame becomes strong and unflickering. This is the flame of truth. Ask it what you should do. Slowly draw your attention back to the outside world and gently open your eyes. You now will probably find that you have a good response.

Energized heart chakra

309

In yogic thought, the energy center sited around the breastbone relates to the ability to accept and extend feelings of love and compassion.

Focusing on this energy center also helps to develop a connection to the people and to the world around you, and builds trust and your ability to forgive. Today, sit quietly and visualize this area of your body suffused with healing, green light.

310 Breakfast on avocado

Avocados are a good source of magnesium, a mineral we need to maintain a sharp memory and capacity to learn as we age. Magnesium also helps to release stored energy and deficiency has been linked with attention deficit disorder.

Start your day by slicing ripe avocado onto wholegrain toast or sprinkle slices with chopped almonds or cashew nuts (more good sources of this essential mineral) and add a dash of balsamic vinegar.

Use your opposite hand

311

To start creating new neural connections in your brain early in the day, use your opposite hand to carry out such tasks as opening the fridge door, brushing your teeth and hair, and spreading butter on your toast.

Doing old things in new ways lays down fresh pathways and patterning in the brain, which helps us come up with new ways of processing data, more flexible reasoning and more judicious decision-making.

Wise thought

TODAY'S SKILLS

Rewrite your resumé to reflect the skills you have now, not the ones you had last time you applied for a job.

312 Approach a stranger

In T S Eliot's play *The Cocktail Party*, confiding in a mysterious stranger forces the protagonists to confront the truth about their lives. The stranger warns them that doing so is to 'invite the unexpected, release a new force' or 'let the genie out of the bottle'. It is to start off a new train of events that is beyond their control. Is this kind of daring just what you need to confront inconvenient truths in your own life?

Uplifting scent

313

Wake up your senses and uplift your spirits with the scent of lemon this morning. As you prepare breakfast, slice a fresh lemon and place the slices in a pan with a cupful of hot water. Bring to the boil and allow to simmer for five minutes to release the oils in the pith and peel.

The scent will fill the room and is valued for enhancing concentration, memory recall and rational thinking. In laboratory tests, lemon aroma has also been shown to have helpful de-stressing properties and to counter any depression, making it a valuable morning tonic for the brain.

314 Breathe into your heart

The lungs and heart share the same area of the body and so, since ancient times, great thinkers have linked their functions, teaching that one of the simplest ways to understand the wisdom of the heart is to contemplate the movement of breath in and out of the body.

In Hebrew, Greek and Latin, amongst other languages, the words for 'breath' and 'soul' or 'spirit' are the same, suggesting that when we know one, we know the other. Think about this as you contemplate the following wise words:

If I keep a green bough in my heart, then the singing bird will come.

Chinese proverb

Chant from the heart

315

Sit quietly and guide your internal focus to your heart. Breathe out fully, then take a deep in-breath; as you breathe out, draw your lips together and let the out-breath emerge as an 'OOO' sound. Relax your lips. Repeat between five and seven times, then sit in silence enjoying the reverberations in your chest.

Heart energy

316

Pin up a postcard of a heart, fit a photo into a heart-shaped frame or treat yourself with heart-shaped sweets as a reminder to keep focused on your heart.

317 Hand wisdom

Today, notice what wisdom your hands hold and what they can say about you. Do they flap around in panic or clench in anticipation of a stressful situation? To still yourself and establish a sense of calm purpose, try this simple *mudra*, a hand gesture used in yoga:

Place your palms and wrists together and interlink your fingers and thumbs. Bring your wrists toward the bottom of your ribcage and rest them against your solar plexus. Now extend your middle fingers so the tips press against each other. Hold for a few minutes, breathing into the area where your wrists touch your body. This establishes calm and allows you to make a wise fresh start on a task.

Learn the piano

318

Playing an instrument seems to help us become better coordinated, and boosts concentration, self-esteem and sociability. But learning to play a keyboard instrument makes us particularly brainy, research suggests. It involves learning to manipulate each hand independently and to use the brain to interpret two sets of marks on paper simultaneously. This engages many areas of the brain at once, but particularly the parts required in mathematical and scientific thinking. Why not book a taster lesson today?

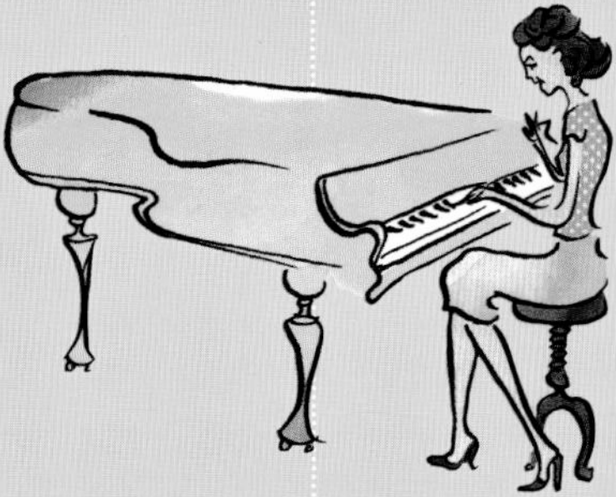

319 Start in silence

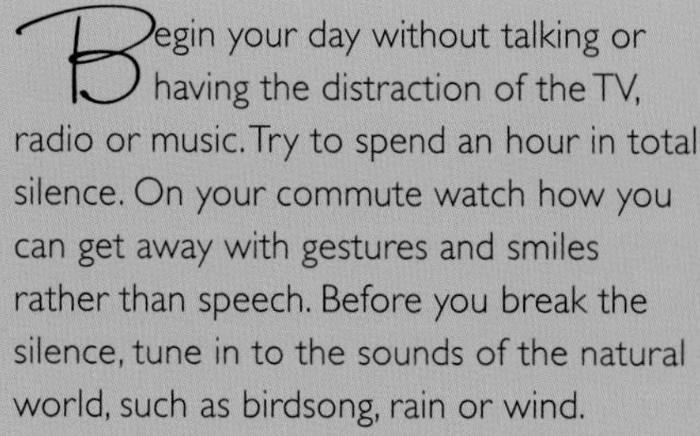

Begin your day without talking or having the distraction of the TV, radio or music. Try to spend an hour in total silence. On your commute watch how you can get away with gestures and smiles rather than speech. Before you break the silence, tune in to the sounds of the natural world, such as birdsong, rain or wind.

It is the province of knowledge to speak, and it is the privilege of wisdom to listen.

Oliver Wendell Holmes

The value of pleasure

320

The journey to greater wisdom should be filled with pleasure. Today, find an excuse to have fun. Take a friend to a fairground, make a den with the children, have a glass of wine after work or put on a pair of heels and go dancing.

Taking a break from the daily grind to have fun keeps the brain acute and functioning well (especially if you tend to overwork), and to promote happiness, health and independence as we age.

Don't tell yourself that you'll do it when you've finished that project; do it today!

321 Celebrate en masse

Wise thought

STREET PARTY

If nothing much happens where you live, get together with close neighbors to organize a street party.

To establish yourself in to your community, grasp any opportunities to celebrate meaningful days for your region and its communities. This contributes to communal wisdom. Find out about the traditional seasonal festivities to welcome in the spring, give thanks for harvest and brighten up a long winter. Volunteer to help raise money for fireworks or organize a mass bike ride.

Supported backbend

322

This yoga pose opens up the front of the body and encourages deeper breathing. Place one yoga block (or use a telephone directory) on the floor and lie back over it, so that the bottom edge ends where your bra strap would be and your upper back is supported.

Rest your head comfortably on the floor or on a folded blanket. Stretch your legs away from you and rest your arms away from your sides, palms upward. Feel your chest lifted and your abdomen relaxed and notice how this relaxation leads to smoother breathing. Rest here for up to five minutes. As you become more practiced, increase the number of blocks or rest your arms behind your head, clasping opposite elbows.

323 Heros and she-roes

The writer Maya Angelou urges us to recognize and celebrate our heroes and 'she-roes'. Who are these celebrities in your community? The childcare workers, teachers and fighters for equality past and present? These are your wise role models and more people deserve to know about them. Spread the wisdom by nominating someone special for a reward, a plaque or a name day to keep their good works alive for future generations.

One great, strong, unselfish soul in every community could actually redeem the world.

Elbert Hubbard

Go to the dance

324

Dancers use their bodies to tell a story, but in contemporary dance there may not even be a story. What can this teach us? Why not book tickets for a performance to find out?

Allow yourself to appreciate the patterns and sequencing, the ways the bodies move around the space, the contrast between isolation and interaction. Notice the transferral of weight, the way the dancers release and balance and use tension and relaxation to engage your emotions. What wisdom does this give you?

325 Who are your teachers?

You may have found a spiritual guru already, but the most unexpected people are also teaching you life lessons. Could it be the student you mentor, your kid sister or a grandparent?

Look out for unexpected gurus today and ways to follow up the thoughts they inspire.

Teachers open the door, but you must enter by yourself.

Chinese proverb

Take a compliment

326

Do you get bashful when someone compliments you on a good job done or a friend says how good your hair looks? That reveals a lack of self-esteem or faith in other people's motives. And this journey toward wisdom is all about belief in yourself and others.

Being wise in your personal relationships means accepting positive comments with good grace. Don't disparage yourself, put on false modesty, make the other person feel small or look for an implied snub. Think about what you've achieved, for example the overtime you've put in. Stand tall, smile and say 'thank you'. Keep an eye out for ways to compliment others, too.

327 Give good criticism

The art of giving useful, wise criticism to people rather than comments that make them feel discouraged is easy if you follow a few rules. Always say positive things in the second person: 'You did that really well.' Follow on with constructive information about stuff that wasn't so successful, using the first person: 'I thought this aspect needed work.' End on a positive note of praise.

He has a right to criticize, who has a heart to help.

Abraham Lincoln

Bathe in music

328

Jazz is the art of improvization: musicians collaborate to make up a piece of music in the moment. You can share in that moment of wisdom by stopping everything to listen along.

Begin with the first track on Miles Davis's album *Kind of Blue*, 'So What'. Become quiet as the piano draws you in, then lose yourself in the thoughts of the moment spun out by each musician.

Take a music bath once or twice a week for a few seasons, and you will find that it is to the soul what the water bath is to the body.

Oliver Wendell Holmes

329 Palm massage

Yogis believe that at the middle of the palms lies an energy center connected to the heart center and your ability to reach out and make connection with others.

Cradle the back of your left palm in the fingers of your right hand and, with your thumb, gently circle this area, working outward from the center and easing out spots that feel tense. Repeat the same thing on the other hand.

Dance away

330

Inspired by the wisdom of dance, today give over 30 minutes to expressing your take on the world through your body. Play by initiating movement from different joints: from your elbows or knees, wrists or hips, and follow where this leads.

Experiment by repeating a single action, but fueled by a different force: effort or anger, lightness or with gravity. Explore the actions that defined your day, such as typing, driving or painting, by weaving them into your individual dance.

To watch us dance is to hear our hearts speak.

Hopi saying

331 Try bibliotherapy

If your journey to wisdom is being hampered by anxiety, depression or emotional difficulties, try reading.

Self-help books have been shown to be as useful as medication in treating mild to moderate cases of these conditions. Ask your doctor or a librarian if they run a books-on-prescription reading list.

Change your pillow

332

If you suffer from insomnia, it will be a struggle to feel wise, engaged or intelligent. Try changing your pillow for one filled with soporific hops. This sedative herb *(Humulus lupulus)* has been considered a herbal remedy for insomnia for centuries. It can help you to switch off if a restless mind stops you from falling asleep or drifting back to sleep during the night. To make your own, fill a small muslin bag with dried hops or add dried chamomile flowers and lavender for extra scent (these are also sleep-inducing).

333 Five elements meditation

The fish in the water is silent, the animals on the earth are noisy, the bird in the air is singing. But man has in him the silence of the sea, the noise of the earth and the music of the air.

Rabindranath Tagore

This evening, as you sit to meditate, visualize your connection to the five elements in the universe.

Close your eyes and focus on your pelvic region. Visualize grounding, life-giving earth as you do so. When you are ready, shift your focus to your lower belly. Here visualize the earth dissolving into a flowing stream of cool water. Now move your attention to your solar plexus, above your navel. Imagine energizing flames igniting here. Then focus on the center of your chest and visualize the point at the top of the flame dissolving into air. Finally move your inward gaze to your throat and visualize sound vibrations here merging into those of the ether around you.

Wise tale: Odin's ordeal

334

The Norse God Odin was desperate to gain knowledge; not just of learning, but of poetry, inspiration, magic and cunning. These would give him the strength to preserve his creation: the earth and its beings. He sent his ravens out to the edges of the world to bring back news, and sat on an all-seeing throne. But this was not enough. He sought the wisdom of prophets and goddesses, and in order to gain knowledge of past, present and future sacrificed one eye to drink from the well of knowledge. And for yet more enlightenment he willingly hung upside down, speared to the World Tree, which extends over all nine worlds, for nine days and nine nights, until rewarded with the knowledge of runes.

Wisdom: *what price would you pay to gain knowledge and how far do you value poetry, creative inspiration and foresight?*

checklist 11 How did you do?

Whether you tried out several ideas this month or just one, you might like to reflect on what you chose to try and why, and if it worked for you.

1. How many activities did you try this month?

- 1–3 activities ☐
- 4–10 activities ☐
- 11–20 activities ☐
- 21–31 activities ☐

2. How many did you repeat several times in the month?

- 1–3 activities ☐
- 4–10 activities ☐
- 11–20 activities ☐
- 21–31 activities ☐

3. Which activities had a positive effect on your sense of innate wisdom this month?

Use the page opposite to make notes about what worked for you and what didn't.

Notes, jottings and thoughts

335 Rise before dawn

The time before daybreak is thought to be the most auspicious for meditation. It's more attainable in mid-winter, but do try to set your alarm 30 minutes before the sun rises and meditate with a view of the sky. This will give you a start to the day that is full of wisdom.

There is no solemnity so deep, to a right-thinking creature, as that of dawn.

John Ruskin

Life without violence

336

Ahimsa, or non-violence, is the first rule of self-restraint in yoga's eightfold path to self-realization. When you get up this morning, think about the ways in which you break that rule.

When practicing yoga poses or at work do you push yourself beyond useful limits? On the sports field do you try to work through injury? Do you tend to be overly harsh on yourself, or are your expectations of your own capabilities too low? Do you hurry yourself in meditation. Do you buy eggs from factory-farmed chickens? Think about how these actions might hinder your journey toward greater wisdom and their effect on others.

337 The act of creation

This morning, before dawn, think about the sacred act of creation that occurs afresh each day, and all the possibilities this offers to create a new you. Allow your own true nature to wake; imagine it as a golden light in your heart.

Color, in the outward world, answers to feeling in man; shape, to thought; motion, to will. The dawn of day is the nearest outward likeness of an act of creation; and it is, therefore, also the closest type in nature for that in us which most approaches to creation — the realisation of an idea by an act of the will.

John Sterling

Make no sense

338

Enjoy being a little nonsensical today. Find a silly poem and read it out loud, make up a corny limerick or nonsense word to describe an everyday action, such as brushing your teeth.

Research shows that being exposed to nonsense sharpens the brain by increasing activity in the regions related to 'executive functioning' and in those connected with visual and spatial awareness.

NONSENSE RHYME
Memorize and perform Lewis Carroll's poem 'Jabberwocky' to a child. Then ask them what they think it means.

339 Be content at work

A man at work, making something which he feels will exist because he is working at it and wills it, is exercising the energies of his mind and soul as well as his body.
William Morris

Today seek contentment at work. Many religious traditions teach that work and higher understanding are one and the same rather than separate areas, and that we can become more spiritually enlightened by engaging in everyday chores and mundane tasks. How so? By carrying out every task with honesty to the best of our abilities; by engaging with co-workers with good motives, by helping others and learning from mistakes; and by finishing tasks when it would be easier to let them go.

Hindus regard this as *dharma*, or doing one's duty according to divine laws, and it is considered as important in carrying us toward higher wisdom as attending a place of worship. So today, don't moan at work; instead see its frustrations as an opportunity to practice right conduct and so live according to a higher truth.

Act confident

340

People who act confident are often mistaken as sage, discerning souls. Pretending to be the way you want to be and acting as though it is already a reality helps to imprint any beneficial thought processes on the mind.

If you lack confidence, begin this process by striding around your home and talking into the mirror as a confident person would. Play out scenes that you might have to deal with later in the day. Later you can transfer these confident feelings to your everyday circumstances.

341 Loving kindness

Wise thought

FEELINGS
This powerful meditation can bring up all kinds of feelings. If you feel shaky, simply concentrate on the first step for a few days: sending loving thoughts to a loved one.

Sit quietly and spend a few minutes remembering a time when you felt truly content and at peace.

Now forget the details, but remember the feeling. Try to relive those emotions. With these feelings of loving kindness in your heart, visualize a loved one, and wish them the same comfort, saying 'May so and so be happy and at peace.'

Now using the same words, send this wish to a co-worker or neighbor; someone you know less well. Then send the same thought, using the same words, to someone you find difficult to be with or actively dislike. This can be tricky; if it's problematic, don't worry. Finally, send your loving kindness out to every living being on the planet.

Who is Sophia?

342

The Greeks translated the word 'wisdom' as 'Sophia' and regarded it as the feminine form of the divine. Sophia is the illuminating wisdom of god incarnate and she may be personified as mother of the universe, the universal creative force of love, light and truth, or the divine spark within us all.

Sophia has been revered by Catholics, Orthodox Christians, Gnostics and Jews. Find out more about her by looking for writings about, and images of, Chokmah, Asherah and Sapienta (all alternative names for Sophia).

Instant wisdom

MYSTICAL MUSIC
Listen to the recordings of songs to Sophia composed by the 12th-century mystic Hildegard of Bingen, 'Chants in Praise of Sophia'.

343 The birth of Wisdom

In this passage from the Bible, Wisdom explains how she came about, telling us that before anything in the world existed, she was there. And that she is still there waiting for us to share in her delights:

I was set up from everlasting,
from the beginning, or ever
the earth was.
When there were no depths, I
was brought forth; when there
were no fountains abounding
with water.
Before the mountains were
settled, before the hills was I
brought forth...

Proverbs 8:22–31

Morning music

344

As you prepare breakfast, listen to music composed to be listened to early in the morning. This will add to your wellbeing and help you make a good start to the day. The music you choose could be a classical Indian raga, folk songs written to be sung on May mornings, plainsong used in morning prayer or Shabbat morning prayers sung by a synagogue choir.

If you like classical music, try Tchaikovsky's 'Morning Prayer', Op 39, No. 1 or Grieg's 'Morning Mood' from his *Peer Gynt Suite* No. 1, Op. 46.

Instant wisdom

SHARE YOUR SONG
Learn a song and sing it to a friend.

345 Simply believe

The essence of true wisdom in the Christian tradition is faith in a phenomenon we should not be able to believe in; an act that breaks the rules of nature and contradicts everything we know is logically possible, such as the Virgin Birth or the Resurrection.

These miracles cannot be proven by science, and although a wealth of interpretations can be arrived at through intellectual struggle, they all contain clear contradictions and limitations. Miracles only gain meaning through faith.

Random act of kindness

346

When you are out today, do something kind for someone you don't know without expecting a reward. Leave a book on the bus with a note saying 'A present for the finder'. Pay someone's fare on public transport. Give a bunch of flowers to someone who looks sad. Don't wait around to be thanked.

Worship with others

347

Going to a place of worship regularly makes people feel less stressed and keeps them active mentally and physically into old age. How do you share your notion of the sacred with others? Find out about your church, temple or mosque and see how it feels to join in.

348 Learning forgiveness

Asking for forgiveness and forgiving others is demanding but ultimately transforming, bringing great wisdom and peace. When we hold on to grudges, we constantly relive hurtful emotions and see ourselves as victims and this creates a mindset that affects every relationship we have. To forgive unburdens us, by releasing us (and those we love) from that endlessly replayed anger, hatred and aggression. It frees us to step out into the present and use the lessons we have learned to create a wiser future. Who can you forgive today?

If we could read the secret history of our enemies we should find in each man's life sorrow and suffering enough to disarm all hostility.

Henry Wadsworth Longfellow

Awaken your palate

349

Before eating, awaken your palate with some gentle humming. Sit in stillness with your lips gently sealed and breathe out fully, then take a deep in-breath. As you breathe out, hear the exhalation vibrating around your palate, teeth, your jaw and cheekbones as an 'MMM' sound. Repeat between five and seven times, then sit in silence, enjoying the reverberations.

350 Stop reading tips books

Short, bite-sized tips are so great because they are easy to digest and galvanize us into action. However, it is tempting, when reading these kinds of books, not to act on the suggestions because tomorrow always brings another thought or opportunity for change.

So after reading this book, make your next choice, one that focuses in detail on one subject. Read it from start to finish rather than dipping in and out. That could make a real difference to your involvement in a subject, and bring lasting wisdom.

Mantra for the day

The founder of the Methodist Church, John Wesley, taught that we were created with an innate understanding of perfect wisdom, and the freedom to live according to it, or not.

If you choose to follow the path, there's no better way than to live according to these rules, set out by John Wesley in the 18th century:

> Do all the good you can,
> By all the means you can,
> In all the ways you can,
> In all the places you can,
> At all the times you can,
> To all the people you can,
> As long as ever you can.
>
> John Wesley

352 Try a Quaker Meeting

You don't have to be a Quaker to attend a Quaker Meeting. Many who value silence and stillness find their way there and gain in spiritual understanding, peace and strength from sitting in silence with others. Find out if there is a Meeting near you. In a meeting of 'Friends', people sit in silent worship, believing that each individual experiences God directly, both within and in relationship with others and the world. Many Quakers express this by working for human rights and peace.

The silence we value is not the mere outward silence of the lips. It is a deep quietness of heart and mind, a laying aside of the preoccupation with passing things.

Caroline Stephen

Write a haiku

353

A haiku is a very short poem that expresses the 'nowness' of a moment, often by describing the fleeting beauty of a natural phenomenon such as light on moving leaves. Try writing one today.

To enter the state of mind that produces a haiku, let yourself become very still and quiet inside (why not try using one of the breathing techniques in this book?), then string together three lines of words of five, seven then five syllables that describe the scene in front of you. Don't be overly intellectual; it's far more effective to use simple words and to choose concrete images over abstract ideas.

Such stillness
the shrill of
a cicada
pierces rock.

Basho

354 Pass on your knowledge

Teaching is the highest form of understanding.

Aristotle

Today, teach someone, perhaps a child, how to cook a simple dish from scratch. By doing this you can feel good about handing on some of your wisdom to someone else. An omelette or a pancake is a good recipe to start off with because it's instant and although it involves intense interaction and concentration, even quite small children can make them successfully. Try talking about where the ingredients come from and about the transformation of raw materials into something hot, tasty and fresh.

Light a fire

355

Arrange to have a campfire evening, inviting your favorite people to get together to build the fire with you. Make sure that you have enough places for everyone to sit comfortably around the embers, discussing the year that's gone and ways to influence the future for the best.

Ask everyone to bring along a piece of paper describing something in the year they would like to be rid of. Ceremonially cast the pieces onto the fire.

356 Boggle your mind

In Zen Buddhism, students are given a *koan*, a nonsensical or paradoxical sentence, to contemplate until an answer arrives. The aim is to befuddle the rational mind and its ability to reason and work out logical answers.

The student thinks so profoundly and contemplates so many possible answers that the mind becomes exhausted, allowing the true answer to emerge from within. Try it yourself with this *koan*: 'What is the color of wind?'

The more you know the less you understand.

Tao te Ching

Spend time with elders

357

People who have been around for decades most likely have answers to some of life's difficulties, or know which questions to ask.

Make plans to spend time with grandparents or volunteer to work at a home for older people. Is there a memory project or community archiving scheme you can help out with, involving activities like memory gardening, memory boxes or reminiscence rooms? Talk to older people about what makes a happy marriage and a contented life.

What an elder sees sitting; the young can't see standing.

Gustave Flaubert

358 Write your future

Leaf through this book again and your meditation and dream journals, daily notebooks and sketchpads. List the ten most eye-opening things you have done this year. Which will you incorporate into your life regularly after finishing this book?

List the ideas that you didn't get on with. Now you are at the end of your journey could you have another go? With this life audit in mind, list your resolutions for the year ahead.

The future is unwritten.
Joe Strummer

Candle contemplation

359

Once it gets dark today, light a new candle and place it in a window for all who pass to see. Setting a candle in a window is a tradition associated with prayers for the souls of ancestors and for family reconciliation, so you might like to spend a few moments remembering loved ones or thinking about forgiveness. Alternatively, contemplate these wise words from The Buddha as you sit in front of the flame, and send out thoughts of loving kindness to all who see it.

Thousands of candles can be lit from a single candle, and the life of the candle will not be shortened. Happiness never decreases by being shared.

The Buddha

360 Bedtime chanting

Instant wisdom

OM

Stick an OM sign over your desk or keep it in the bedroom to remind you of the sense of calmness and connection waiting for you when you chant.

Uttering the sound 'OM' is thought by yogis to tune you in with the essence of the universe and all living beings. Before bed sit quietly, with your spine straight. Breathe out fully, then take a deep in-breath. As you breathe out, open your mouth wide and let the sound 'AAAA' emerge from deep in your abdomen; then round your lips and hear the sound become 'OOOO'; finally seal your lips to let a humming 'MMM' vibrate around your head as the out-breath ends. Take a recovery breath in and out, if necessary, then repeat the sounded-out breath five to seven times. Then sit in silence, enjoying the whole-body reverberations.

Back to basics

361

If you find any of the instructions in this book tricky, for instance the yoga poses or meditations, give yourself a break. It's easy to get bound up by techniques and information and in getting things right. When we do this, we can forget the object of the exercise, which is to still a wandering mind and body and experience the truth of your real self.

*This is true knowledge: to seek the Self as the true end of wisdom always.
To seek anything else is ignorance.*

Bhagavad Gita

362 Ancient wisdom

India's ancient philosophers, the sankhyas, taught that humankind is troubled by three things, which prevent us from reaching the ultimate form of wisdom, self-realization.

What are these three troubles? The material world, other people, and ourselves, but our worst enemy, they say, is ourselves. Don't allow old ways of behaving throw you off course too often. By trying to do good deeds most days, by thinking kind thoughts and by trying to stay calm and poised during times of stress you can keep the worst enemy at bay. This will transform your relationships with others and make sure that your dealings with the material world are ethical and wise.

Mindful cooking

363

Make your food preparation today a form of moving meditation by focusing wholly on the task at hand. Try to engage fully with the act of chopping, stirring and pouring.

Other thoughts will occur, but simply let them be and keep diverting your attention back to the simple act of cooking. This nourishes your soul as well as your body.

Instant wisdom

GOOD FEELINGS

If preparing a special recipe for loved ones, such as a birthday cake, imagine pouring some of your good feelings for them into the mix as you prepare it.

364 Immerse yourself in nature

Wise thought

EXPERIENCE IT!
Don't wear a wetsuit; it interrupts your direct experience of being surrounded by water.

Take a group of friends swimming outdoors in the ocean, or a lake or river. To find a safe freshwater location find an online wild swimming group that recommends safe swimming spots in your area and read their safety advice. There's nothing like being immersed fully in nature to gain a sense of perspective and relief from stress. Since the late 18th century, a long line of writers, artists and thinkers have found nature experiences to be a direct line to wisdom. To explore this further, look at the writings of William Wordsworth, Henry David Thoreau, Annie Dillard and Richard Mabey.

Wise tale: the wise idiot

365

The Turkish fool Nasreddin Hodja was invited to a fine dinner, but decided to wear ordinary clothes so as not to seem out of place. When he got to the house, all the guests were served food and drink except him. So he stood up and went home, unnoticed. He returned in his best garb to be welcomed, shown to a table and presented with food and drink. To everyone's astonishment, he dipped the edge of his sleeve in the soup, urging his jacket to 'Eat your fill, precious coat.' When questioned by the great and the good, he simply responded, 'When I was here in my ordinary suit you ignored me, yet now I eat alongside you. I can only presume that you invited my jacket, not me!'

Wisdom: *those who confound expectation and question social mores may stumble on essential truths.*

checklist 12 How did you do?

Whether you tried out several ideas this month or just one, you might like to reflect on what you chose to try and why, and if it worked for you.

1. How many activities did you try this month?

- 1–3 activities ☐
- 4–10 activities ☐
- 11–20 activities ☐
- 21–30 activities ☐

2. How many did you repeat several times in the month?

- 1–3 activities ☐
- 4–10 activities ☐
- 11–20 activities ☐
- 21–30 activities ☐

3. Which activities had a positive effect on your sense of innate wisdom this month?

Use the page opposite to make notes about what worked for you and what didn't.

Notes, jottings and thoughts

Conclusion

Congratulations on reaching the end of this journey! Don't feel abandoned as you step forward into the New Year. If you have time for nothing else, focus on these easy ways to keep up the good work:

• Actively spread goodwill to all around you. It's easiest to start with those you love, but try to treat even those you dislike with kindness.
• Get together with others to talk, share food and spend time outdoors. Observing nature encourages reflective thinking and a fresh sense of perspective.
• Practice the yoga exercises in sequence most days. If you have no time, simply do the Corpse Pose.
• Notice connections between what you eat, how often you exercise and how well your body, brain and emotions function.
• Make regular time for meditation or silent reflection at the start and end of the day and take mini-timeouts during the busy hours.
• Notice how you breathe, encouraging your breath to become slower, smoother and deeper.

Notes, jottings and thoughts

Notes, jottings and thoughts